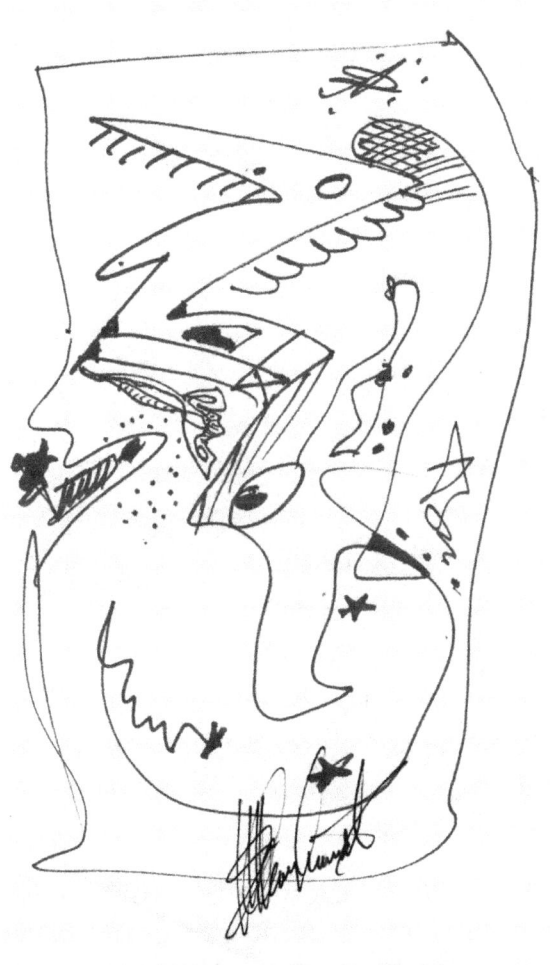

Printed by CreateSpace

ISBN: 978-1722239787

THE ARTISTRY

OF

MICHAEL KLEINSCHMIDT

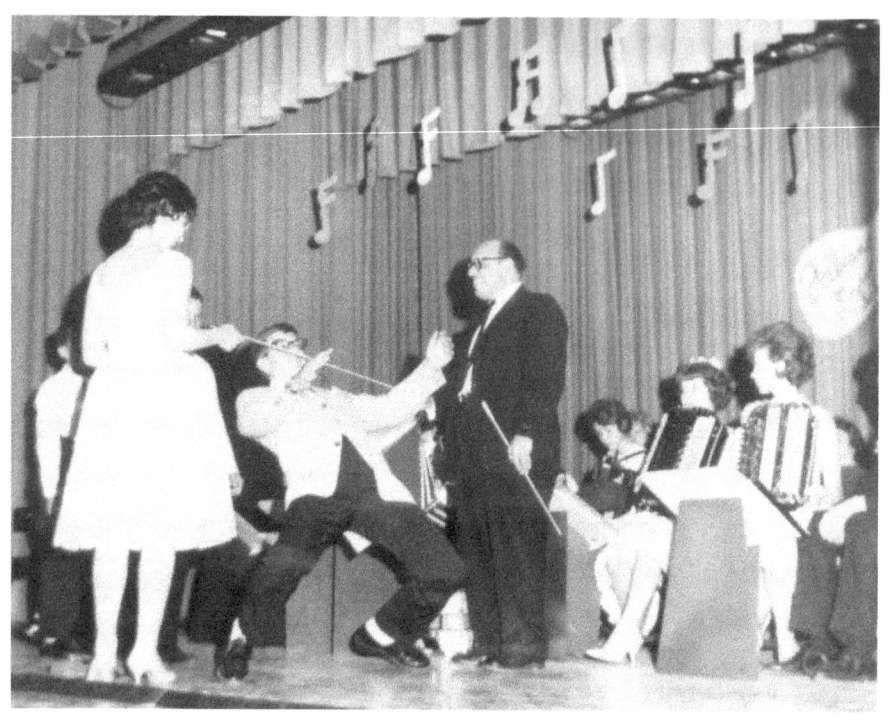

At a young age, Michael Kleinschmidt (1948-2017) became a skilled accordionist and at the age of 17 composed his first tune, *Frustration Blues*. An early love of cameras led him to a job at a television station, where, before long, he found his way in front of the cameras. He was still in high school when he hosted kiddie TV shows as Panhandle Pete and Jungle Jonathan. In college, Michael pursued art, particularly in creating environments and conceptual/theatrical photography. He painted on canvas and board, while design-engineering and welding skills helped him execute challenging sculptures. Cameras and sketchbooks remained constant companions.

This book is dedicated to the legacy he left behind. An artist in every sense of the word, he exalted in philosophy, music, painting, sculpture, photography, theater, prose and poetry, and life itself. On the following pages are select works by Michael Kleinschmidt.

PHOTOGRAPHY

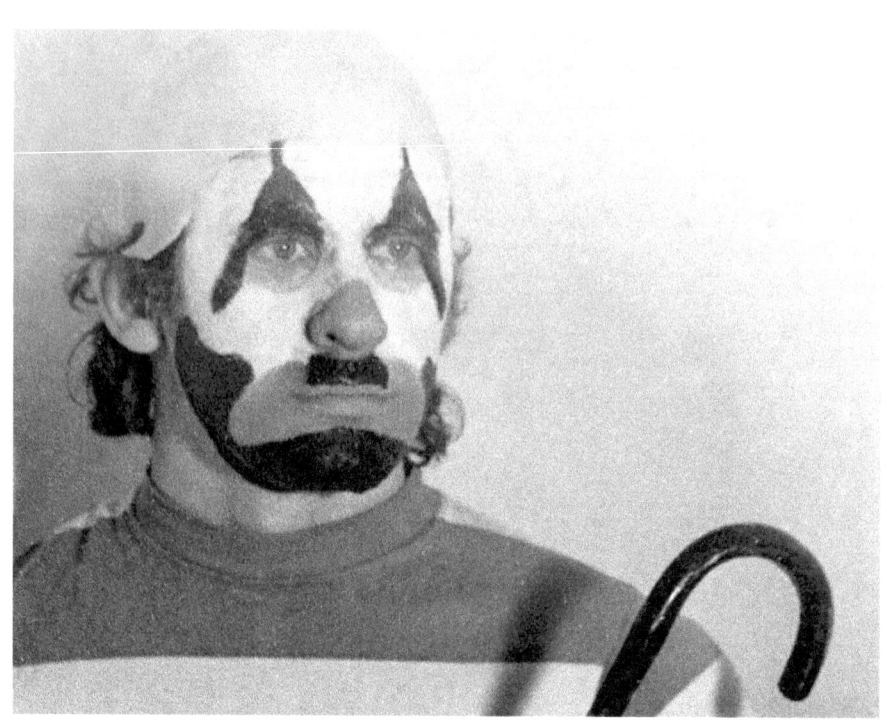

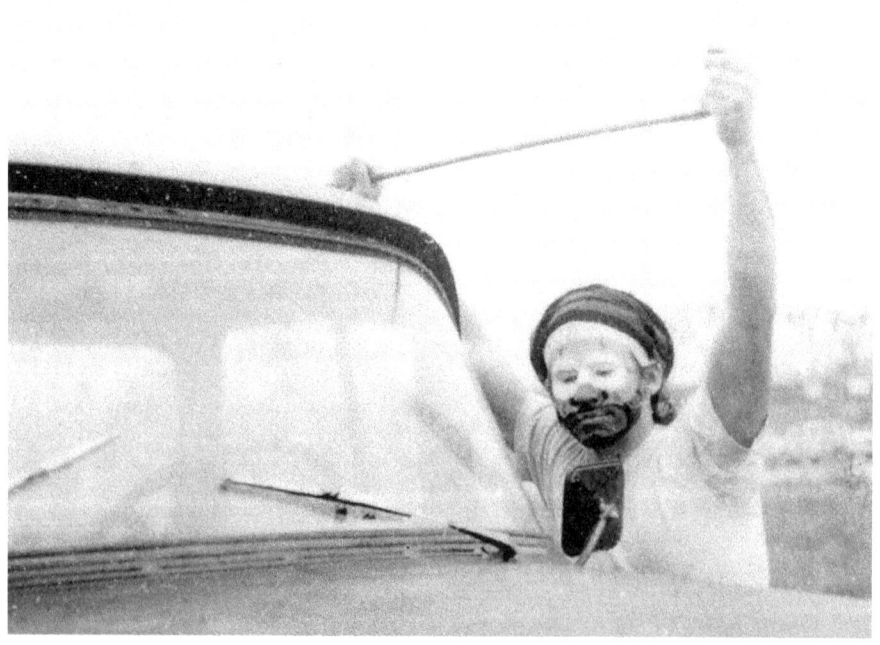

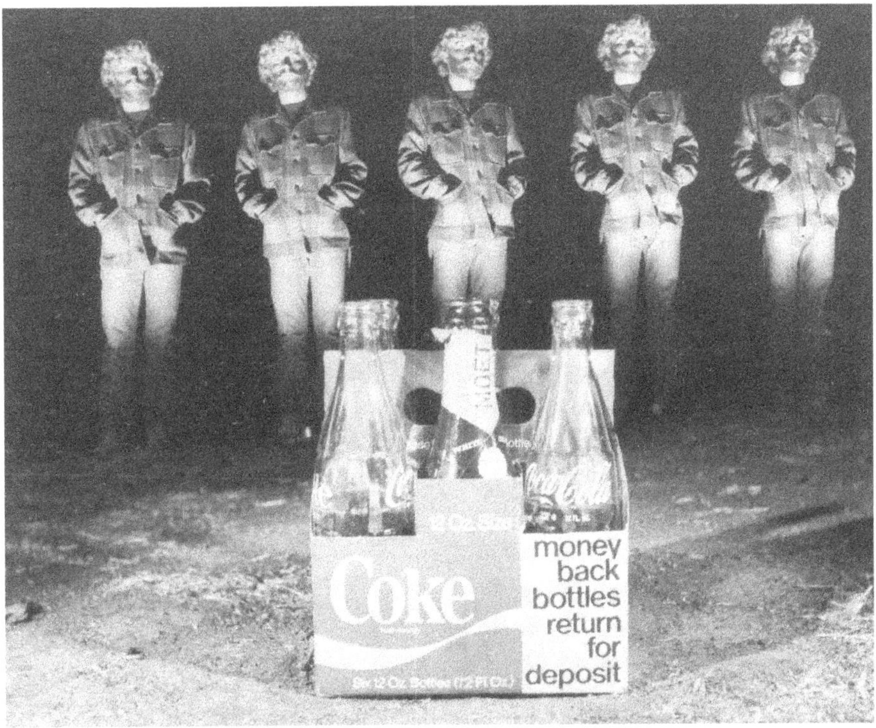

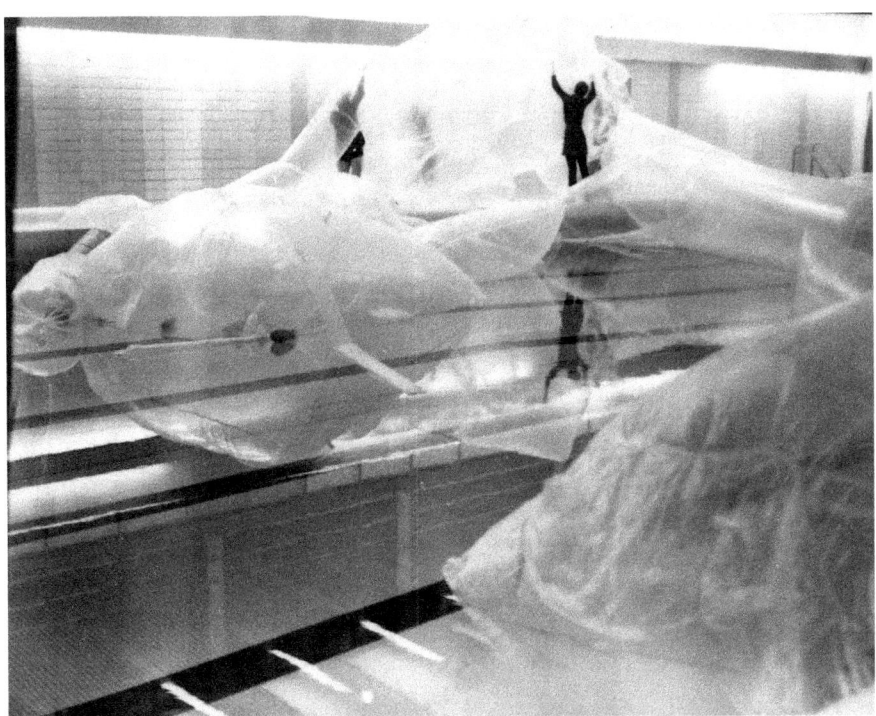

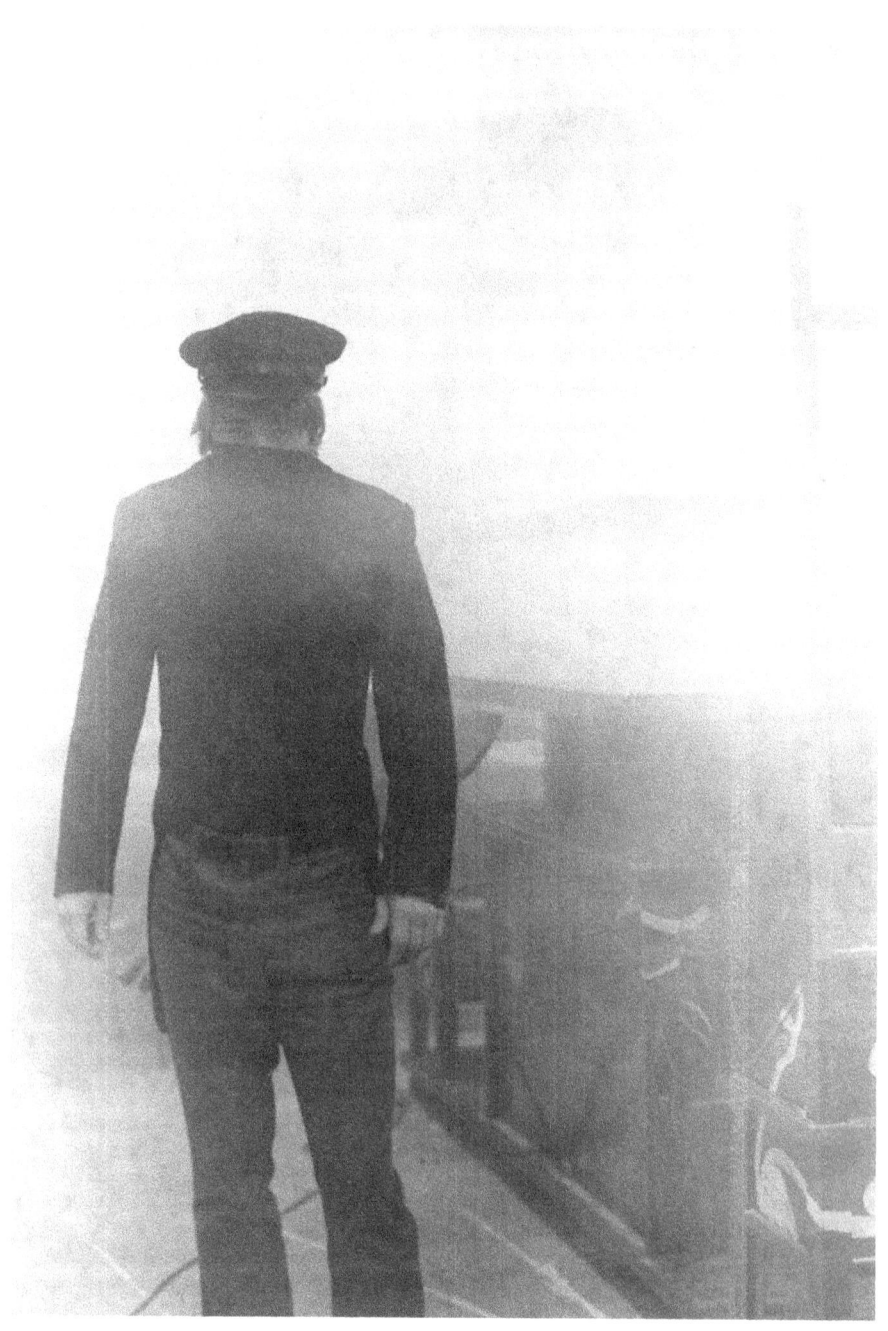

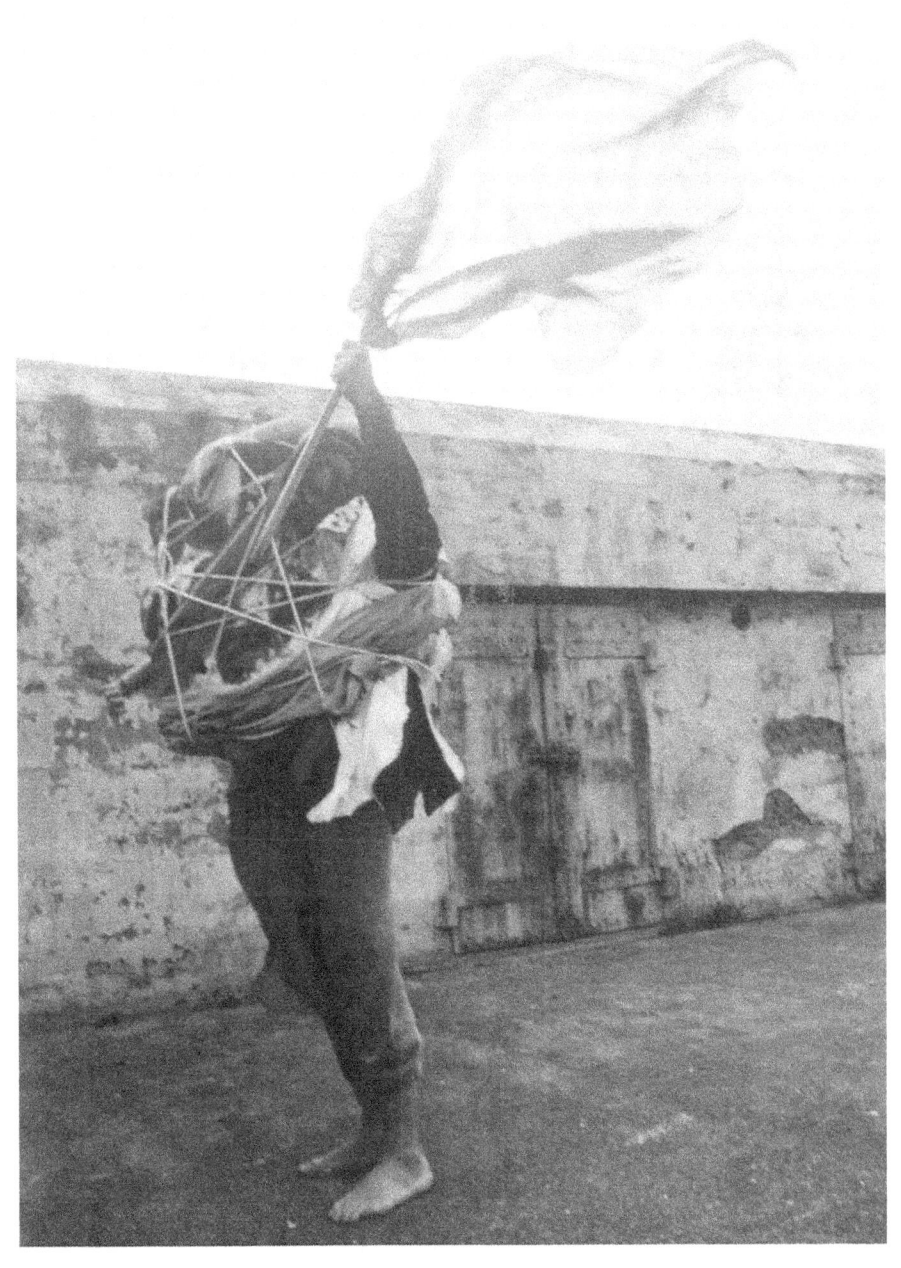

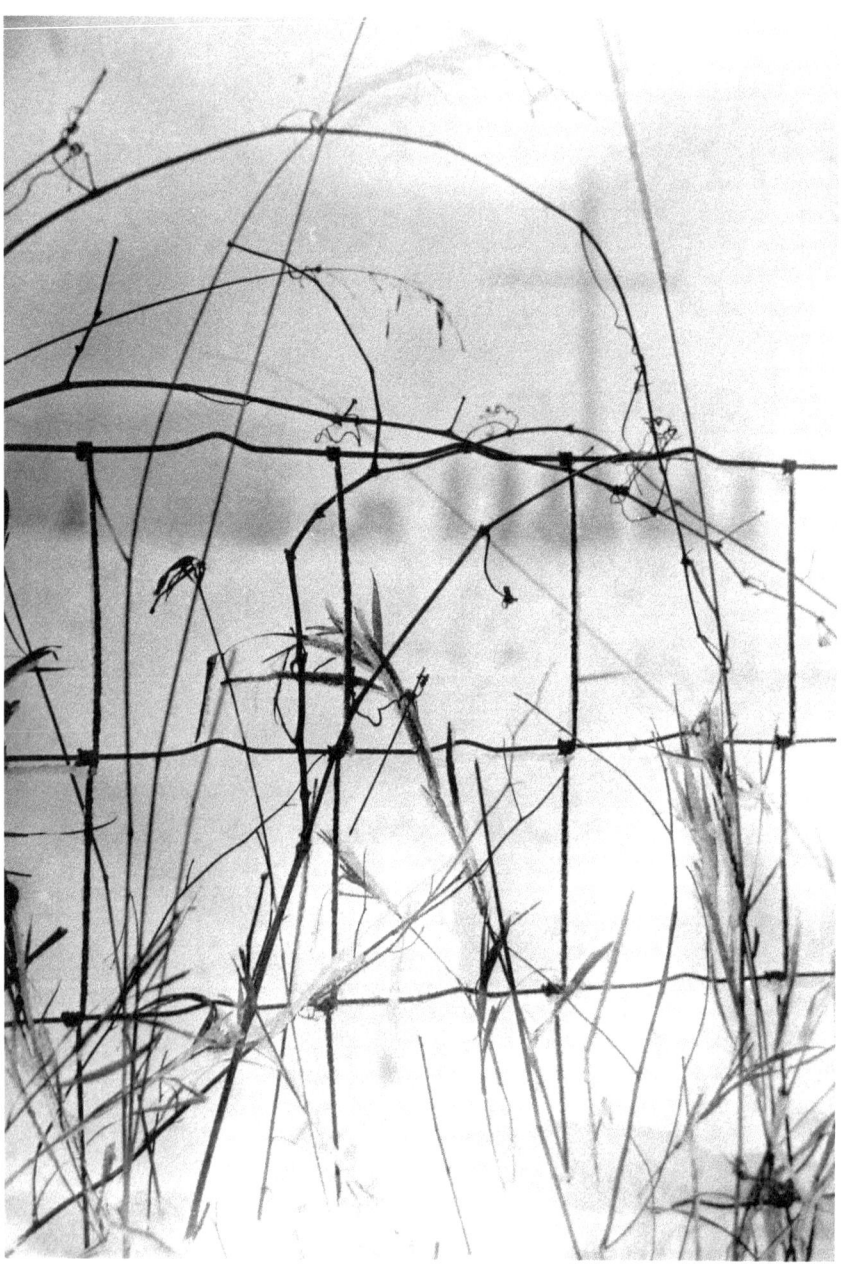

10

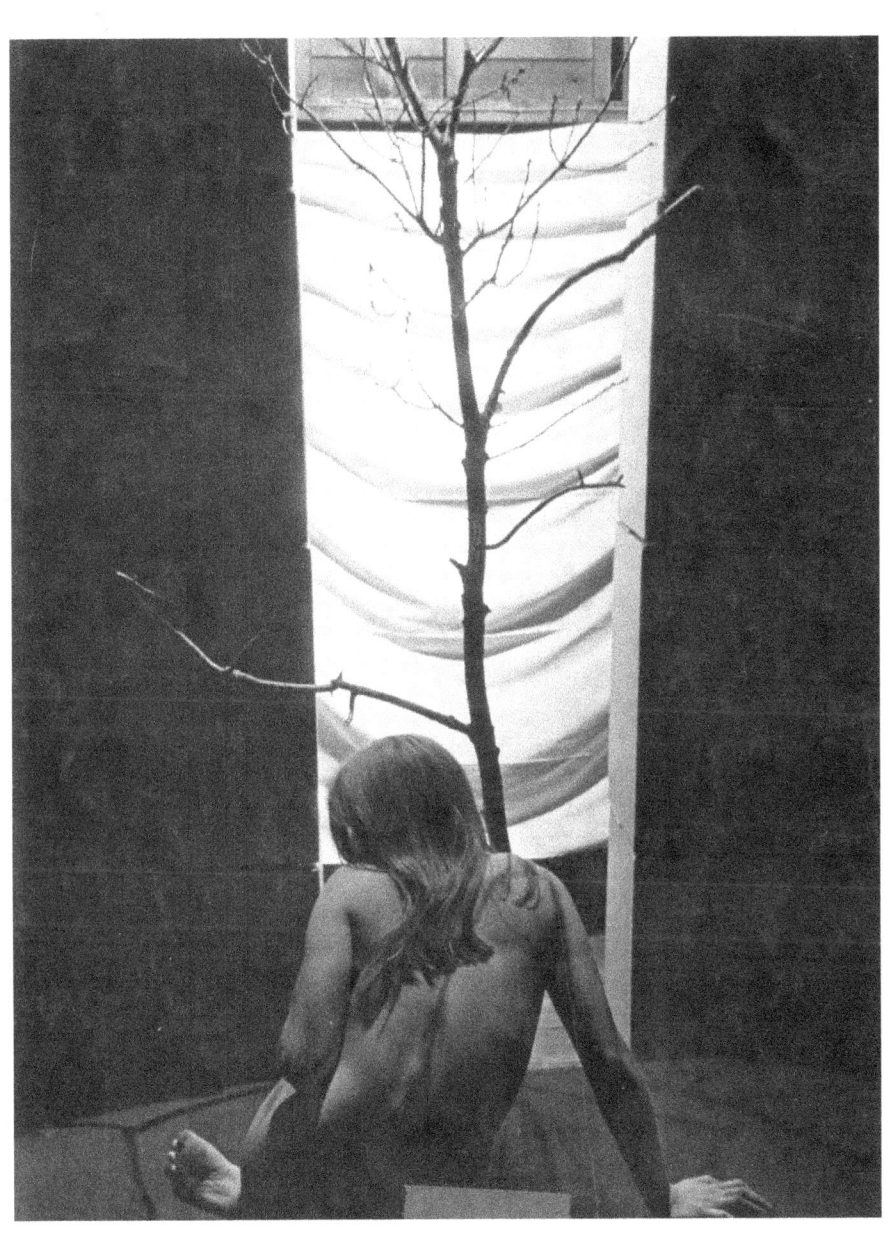

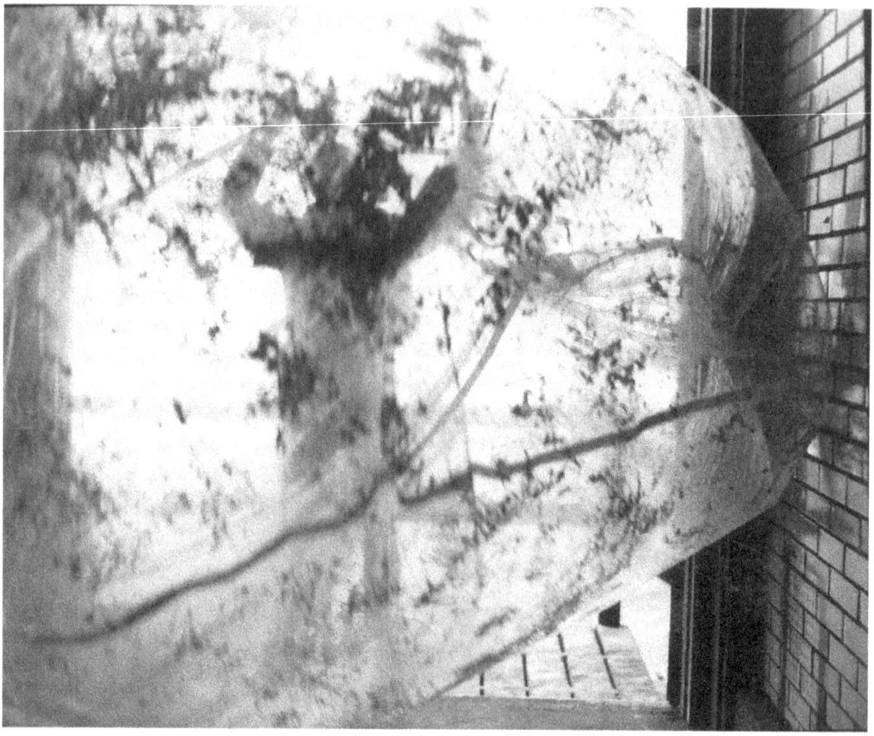

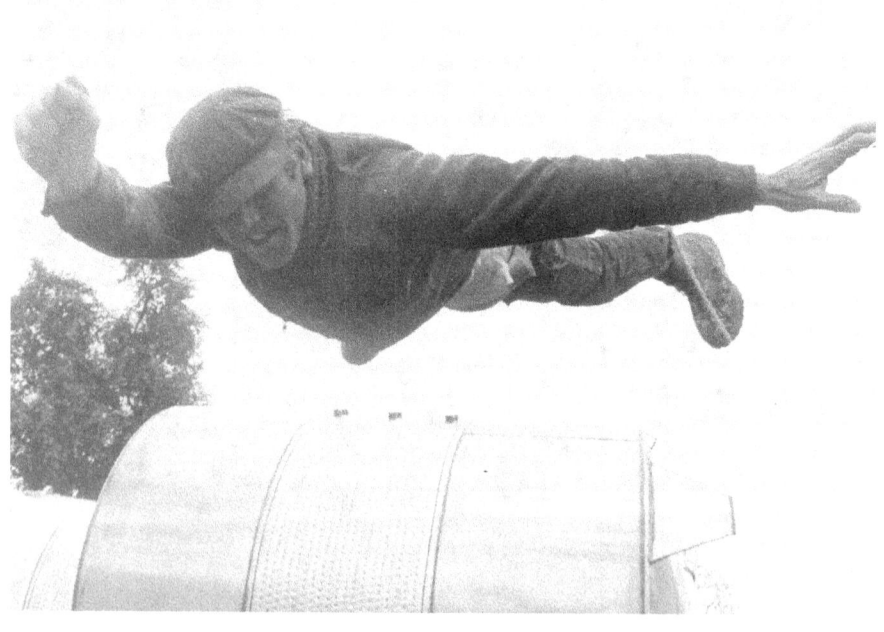

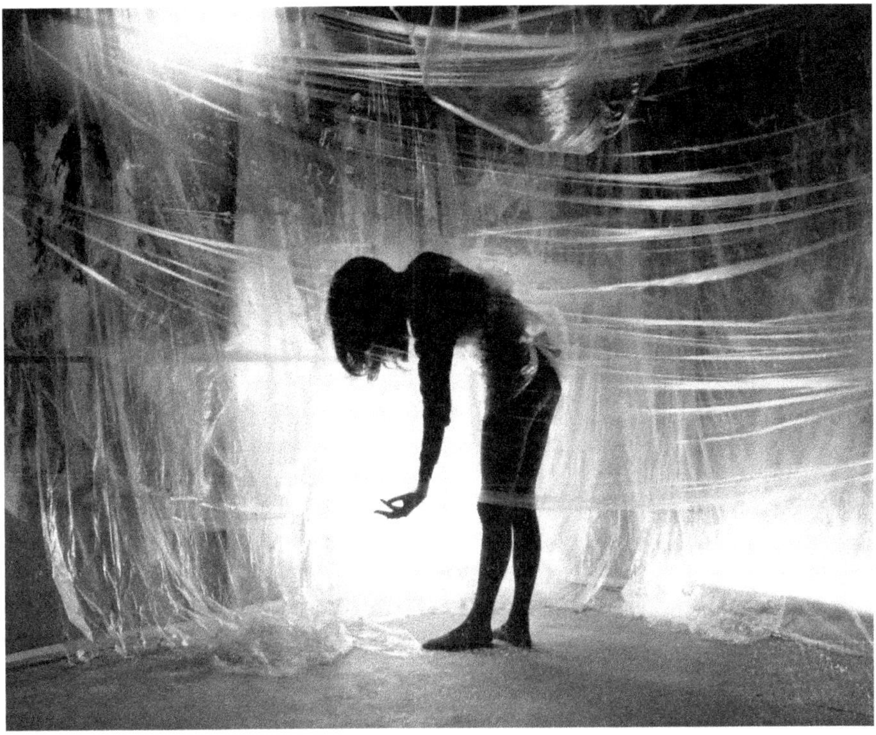

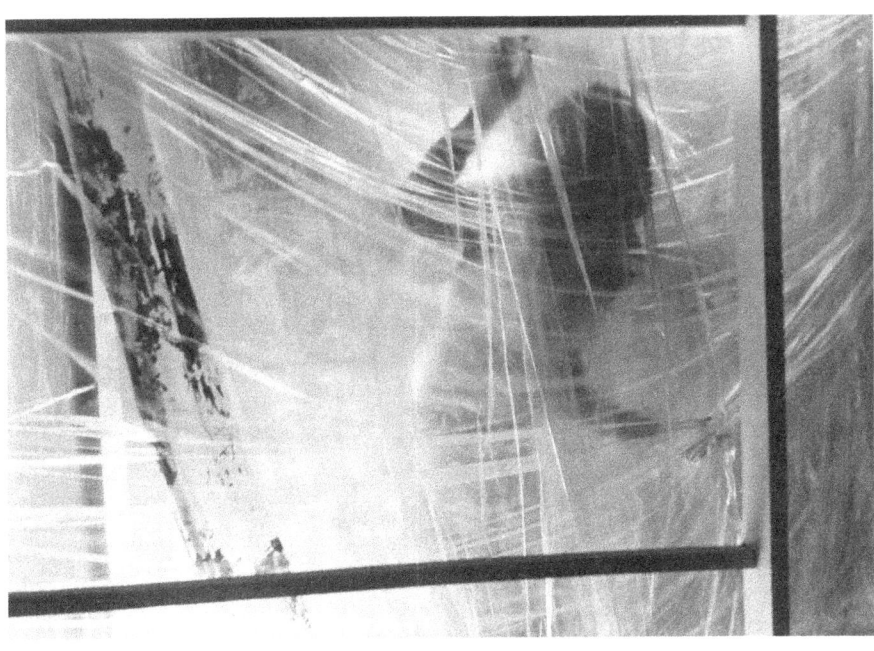

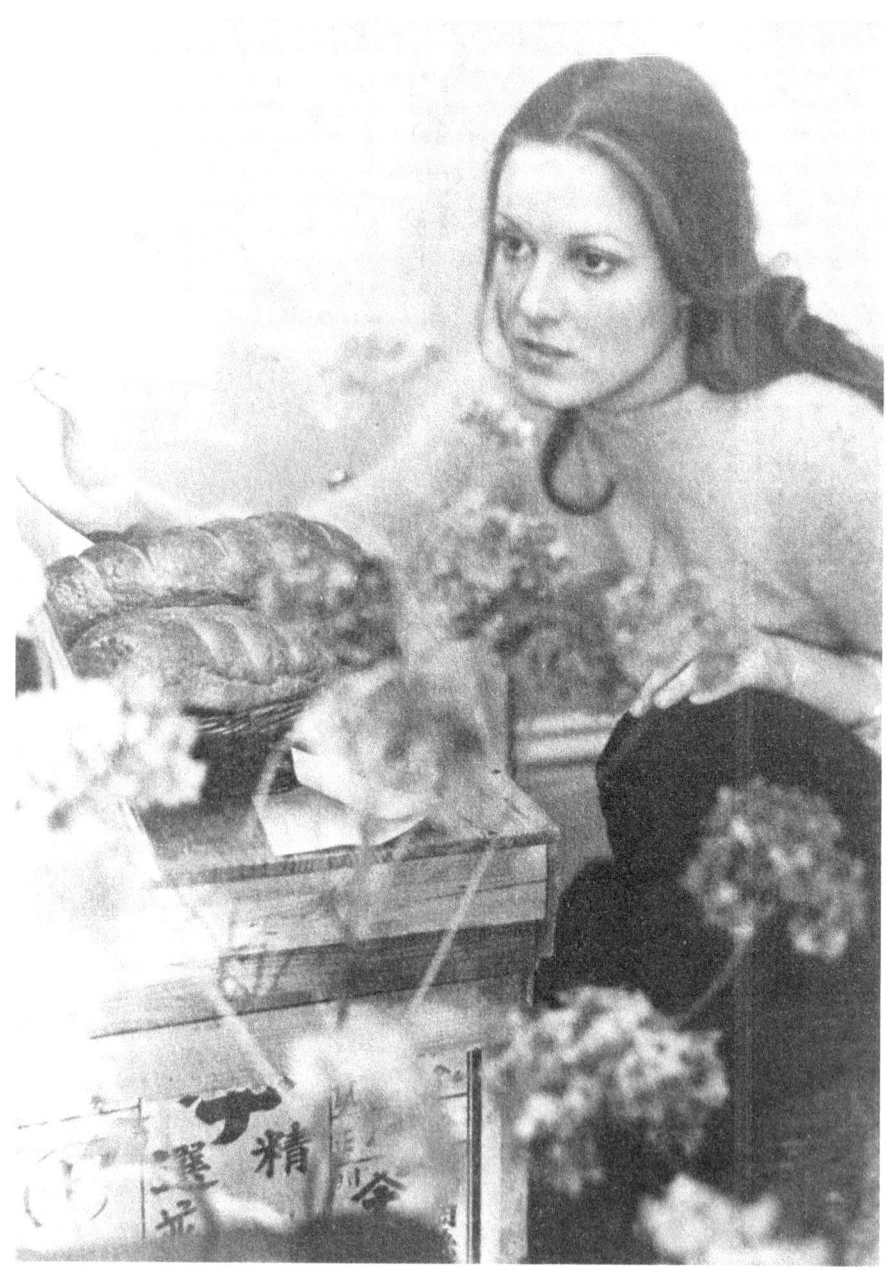

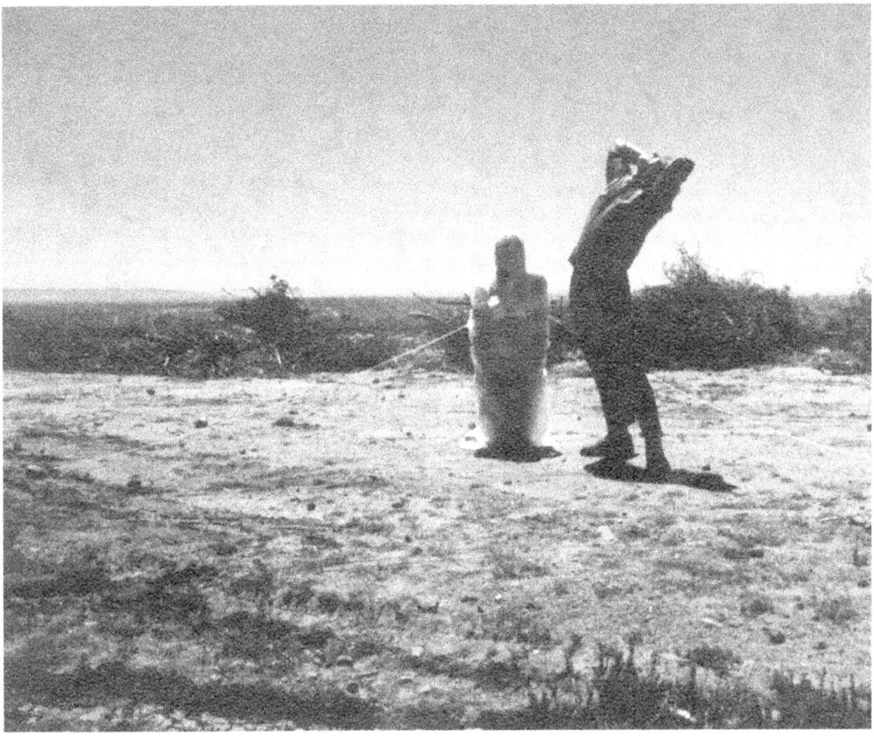

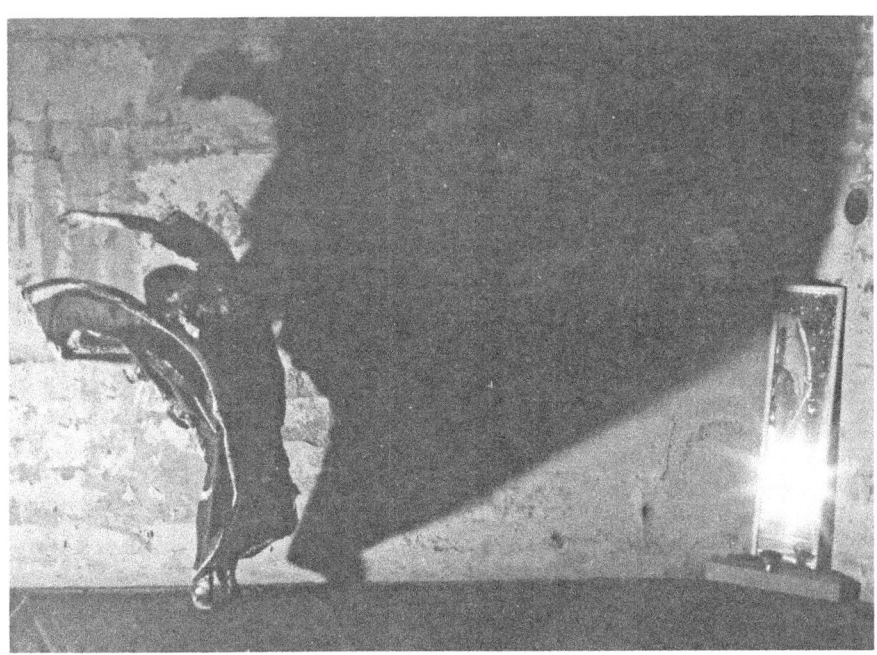

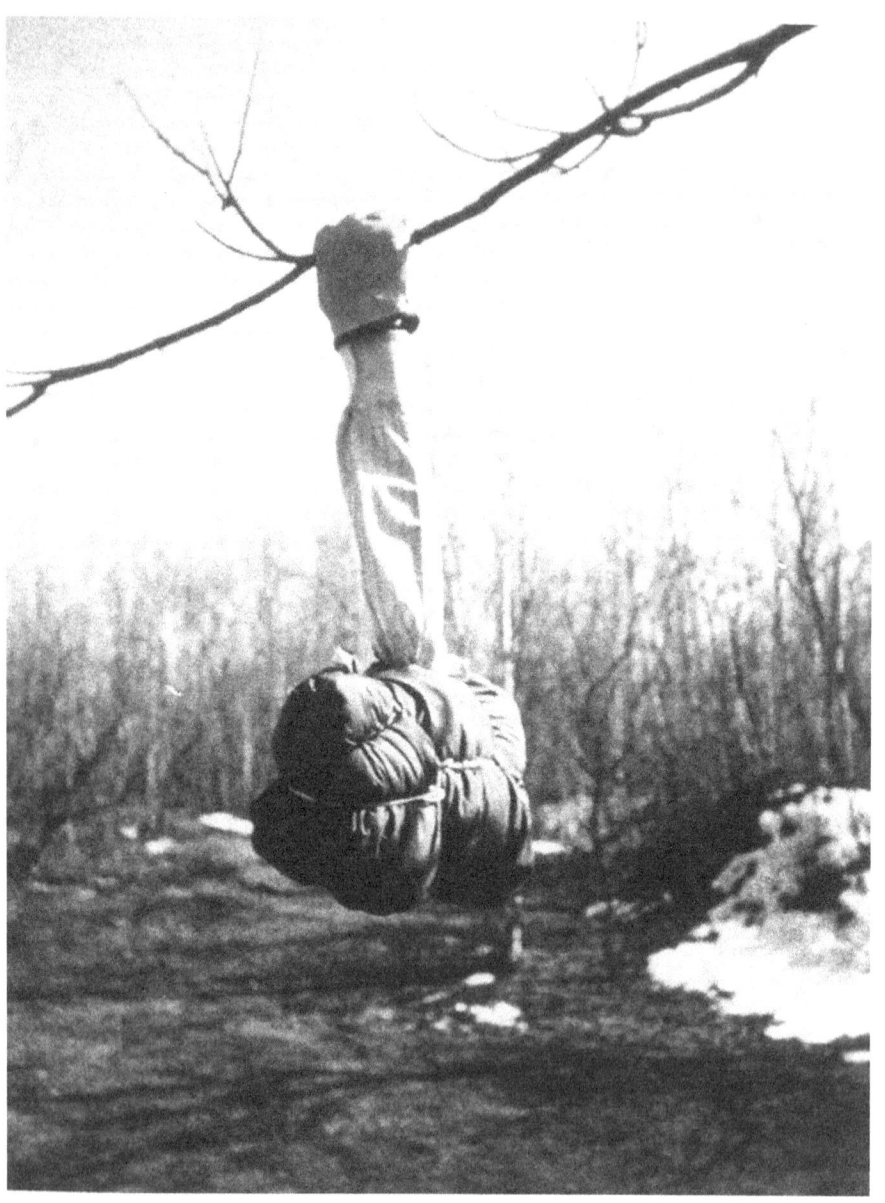

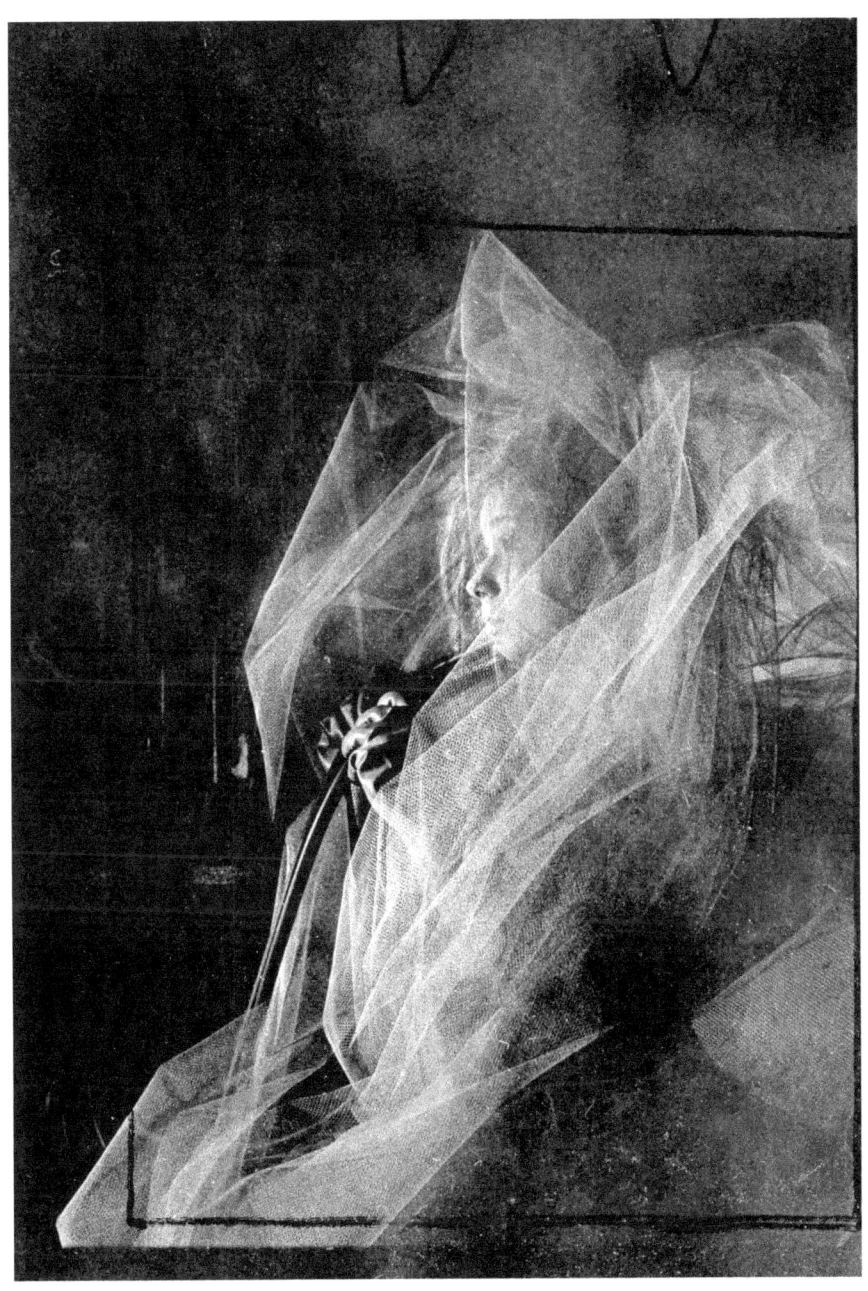

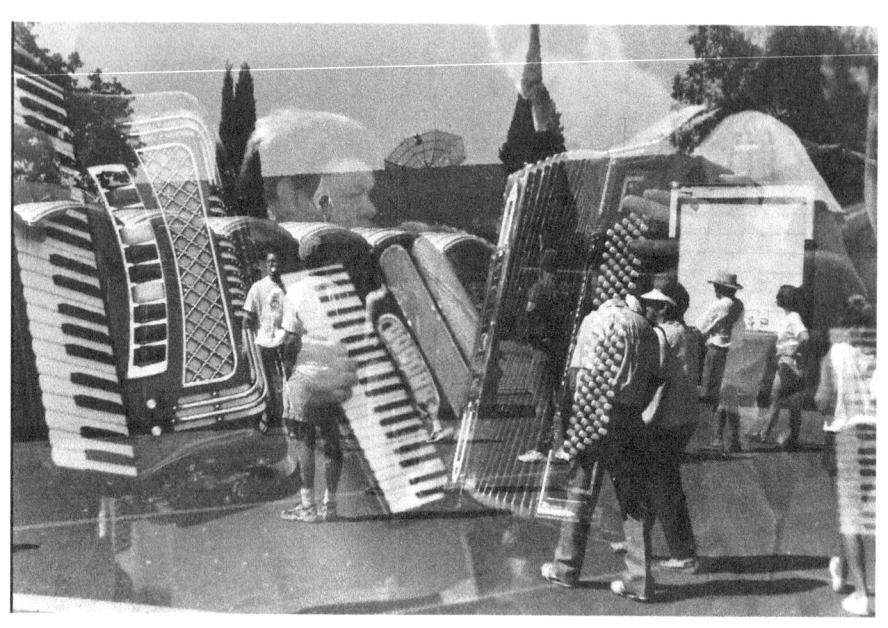

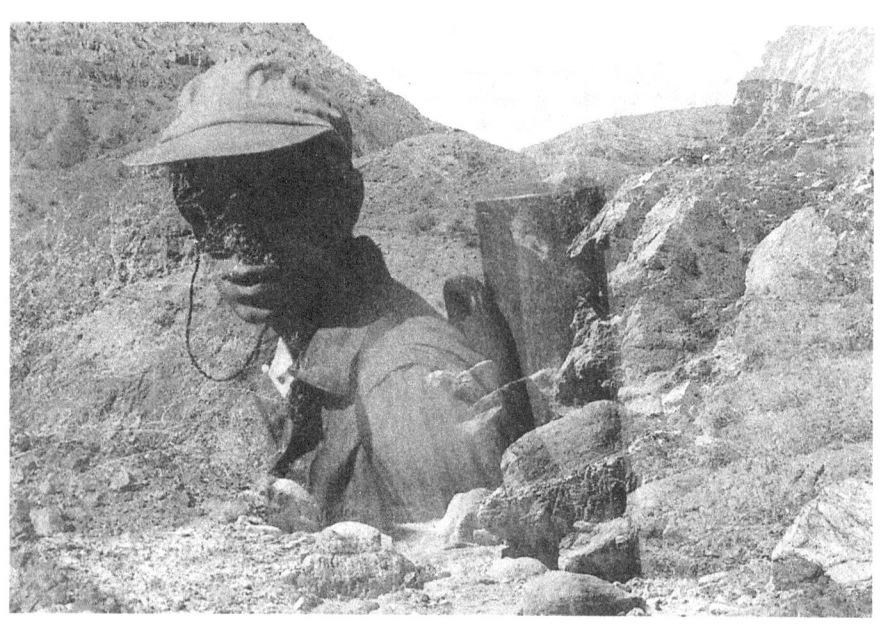

18

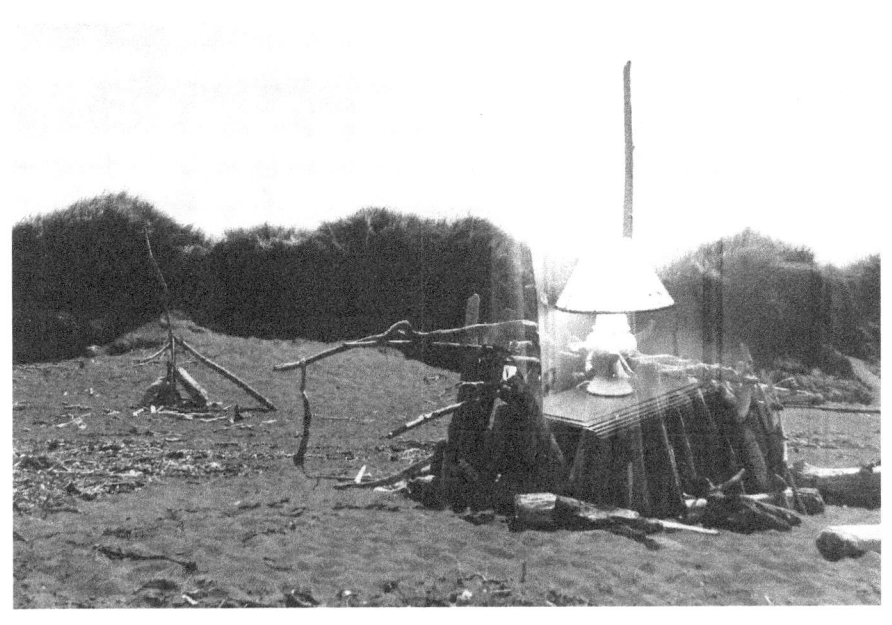

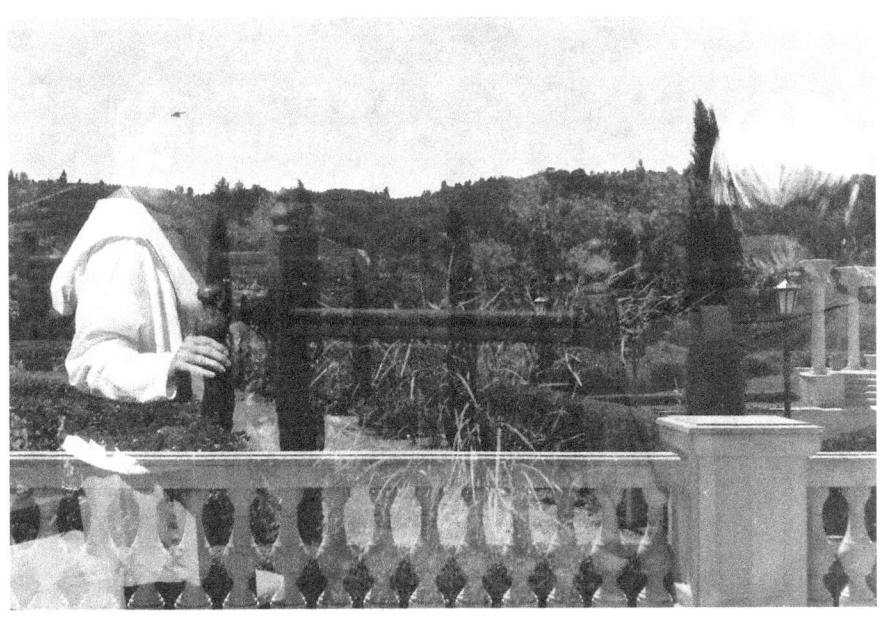

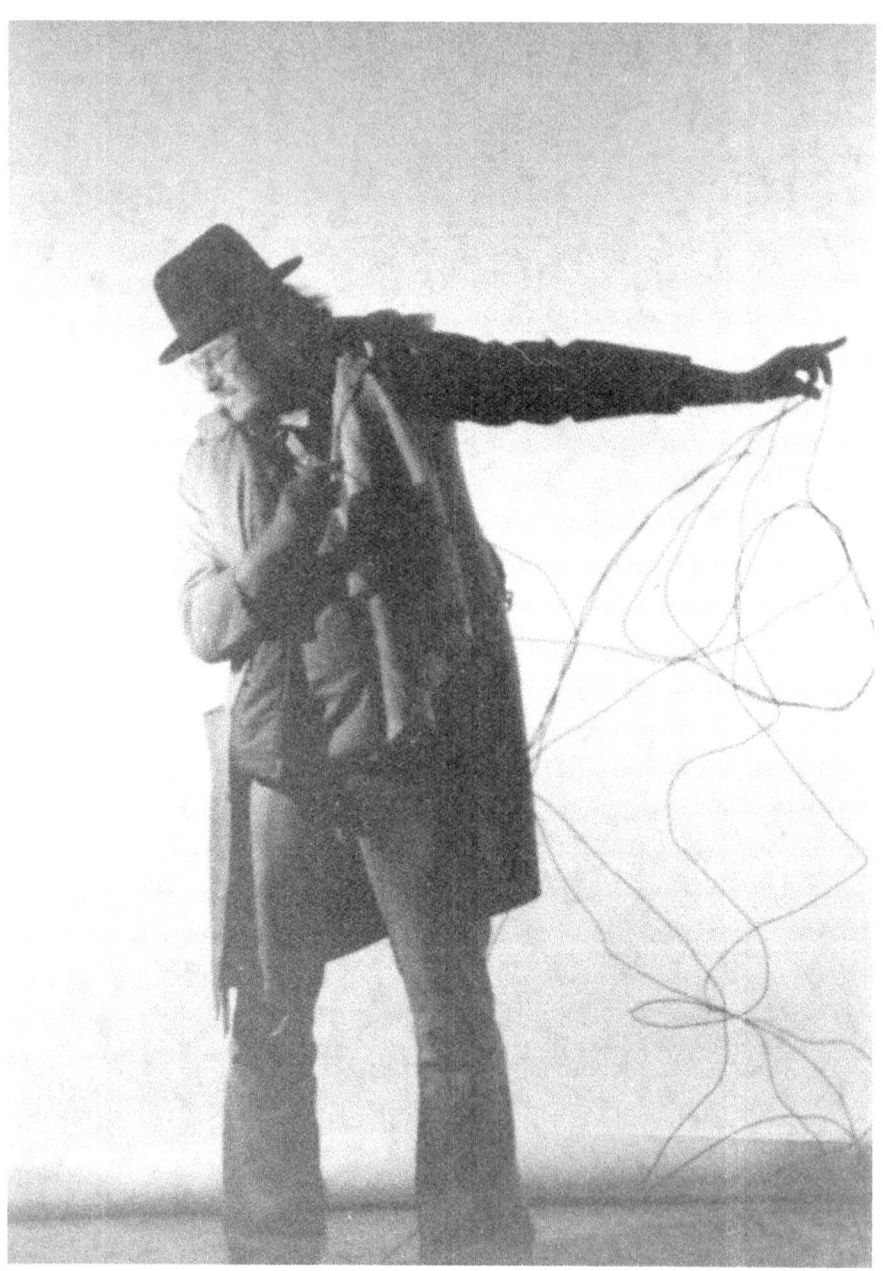

SKETCHES

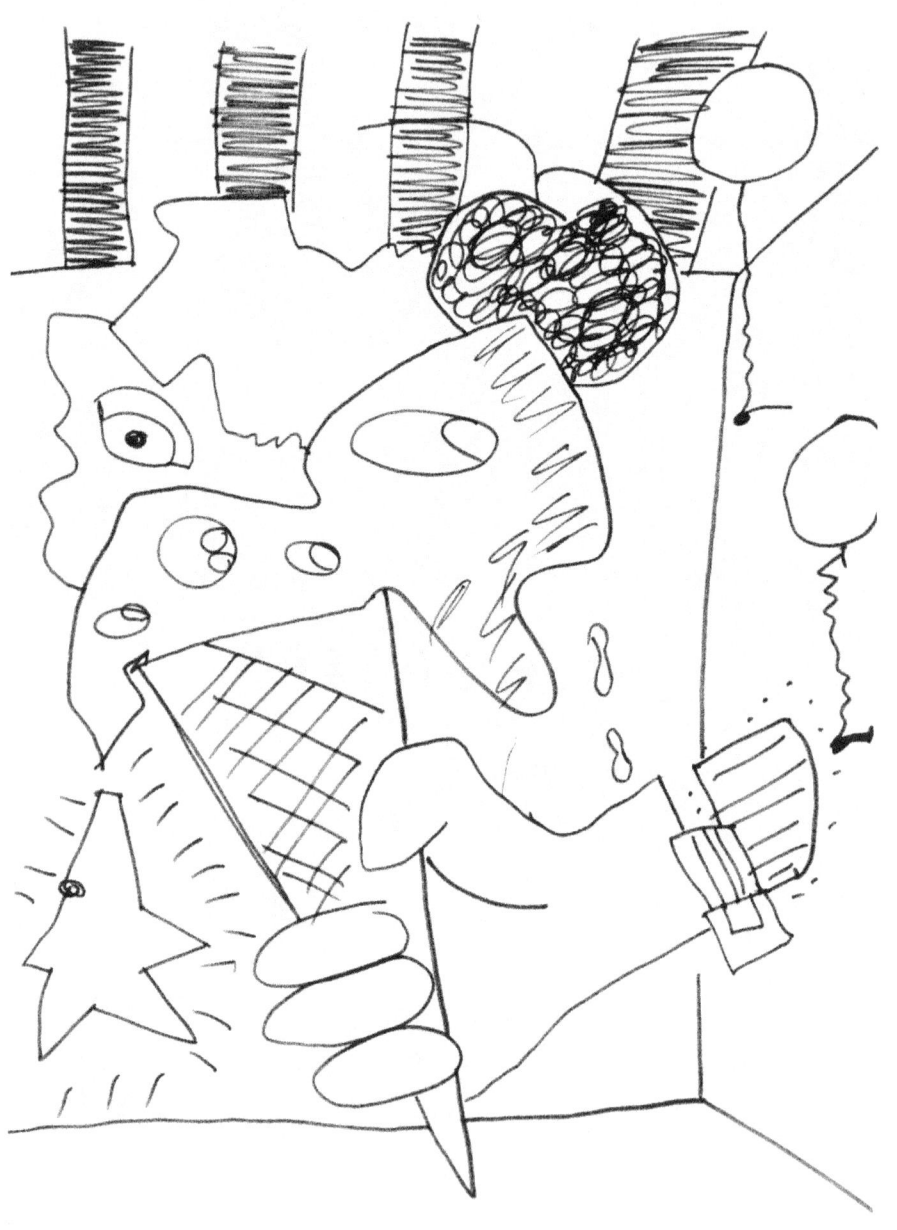

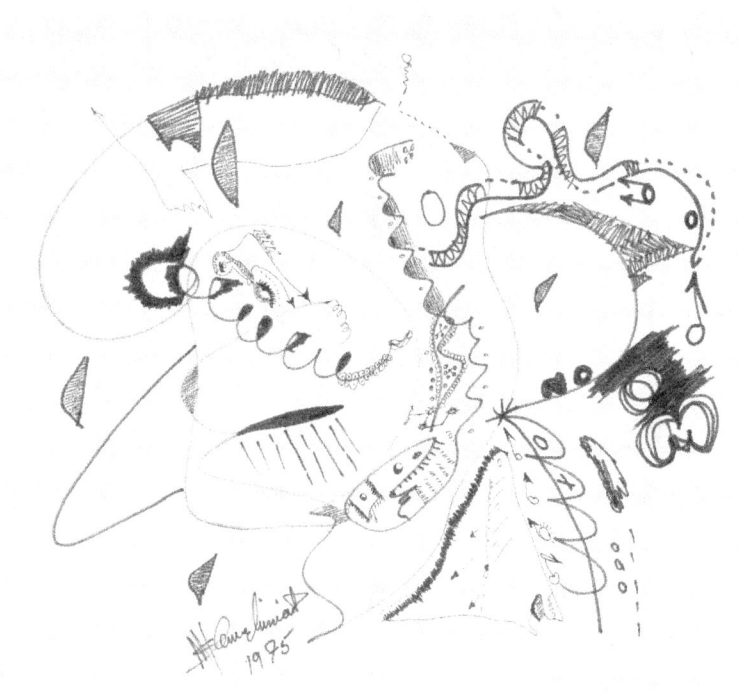

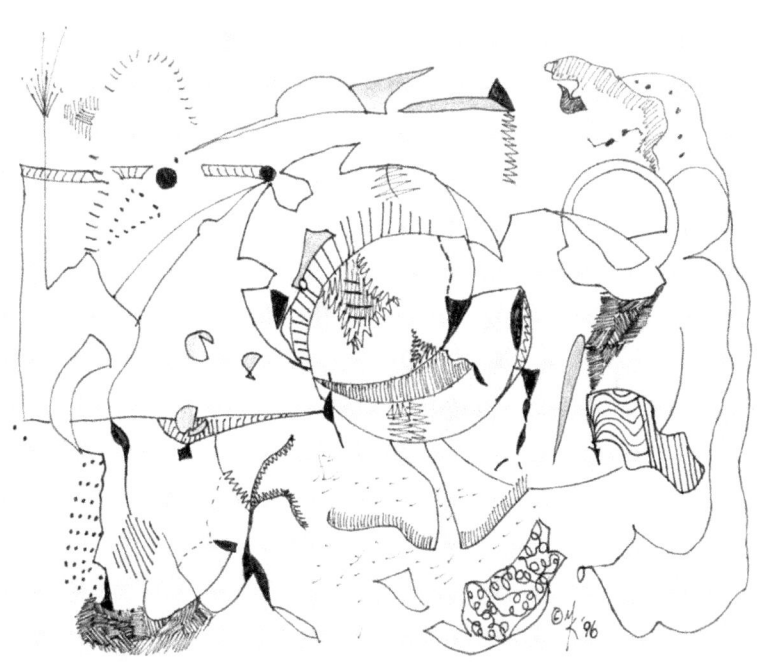

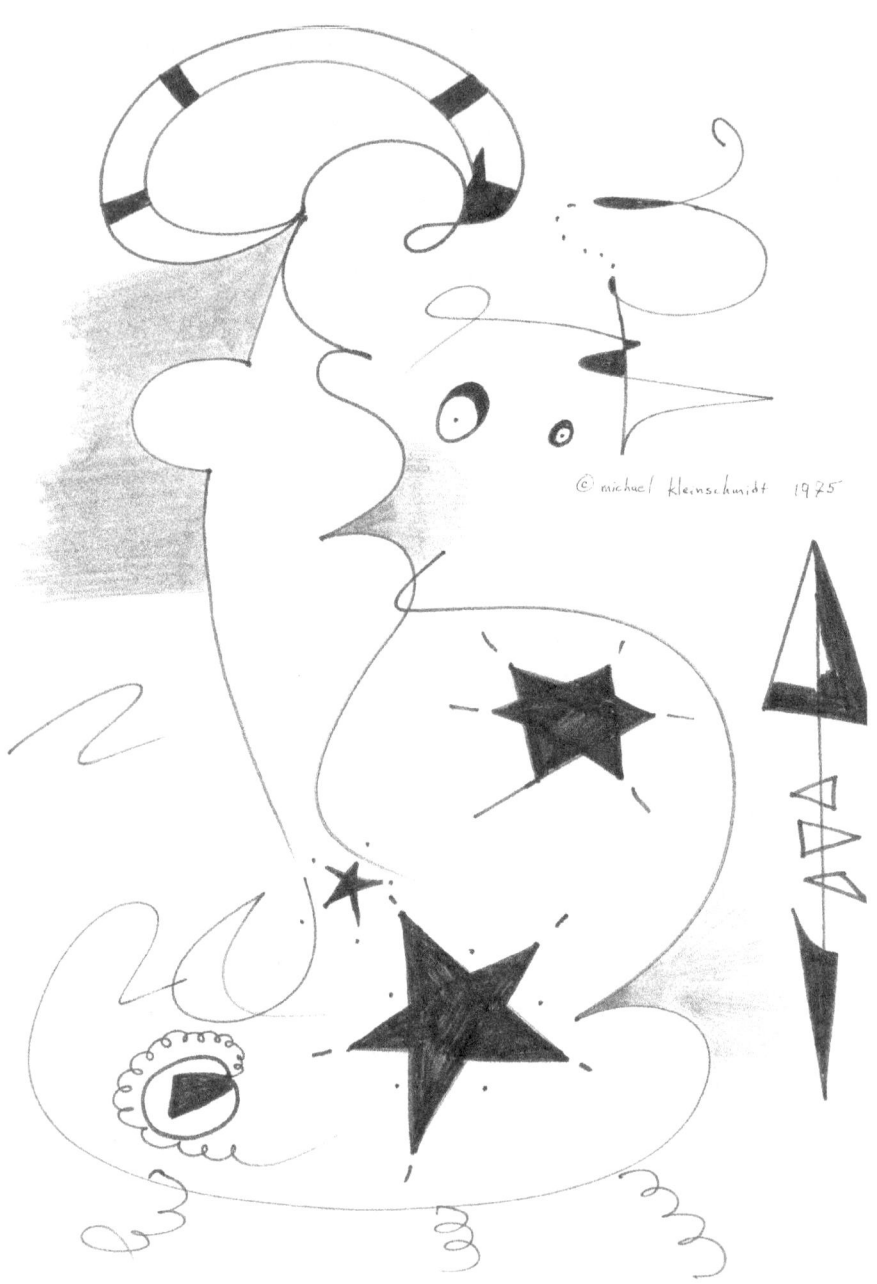

© michael kleinschmidt 1975

24

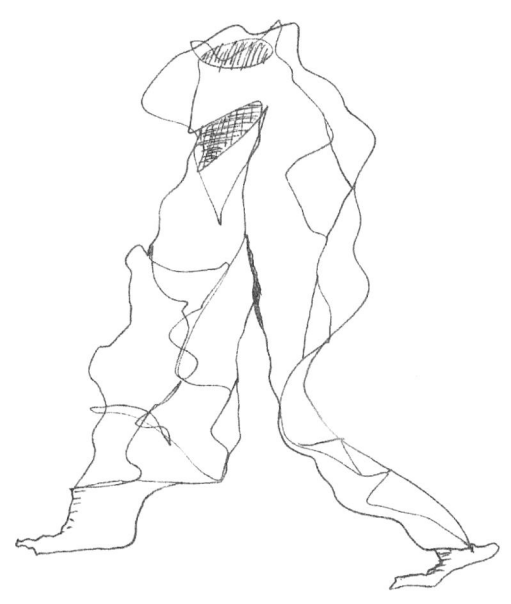

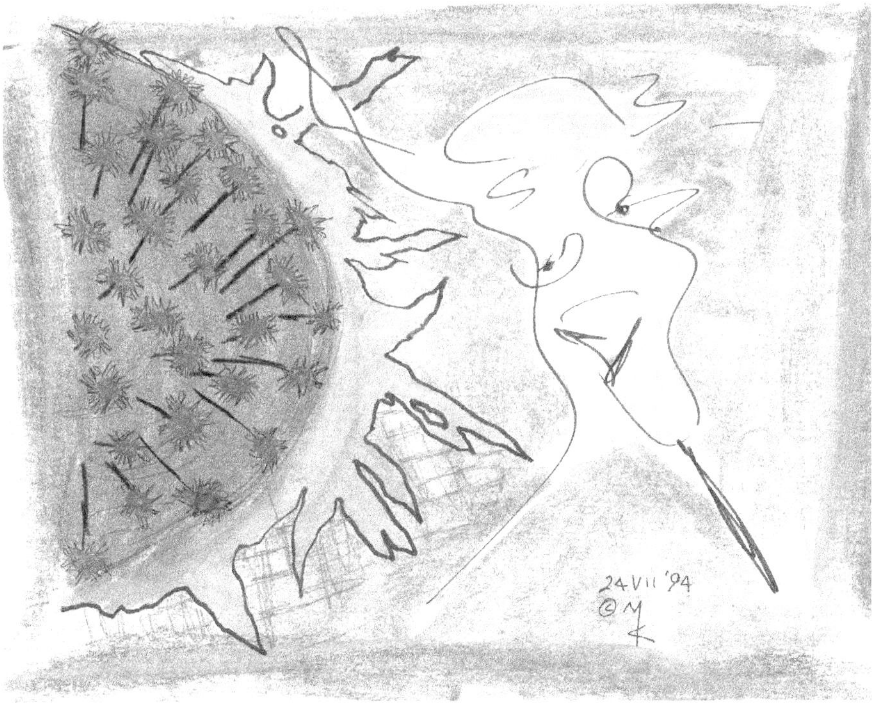

24 VII '94
©M

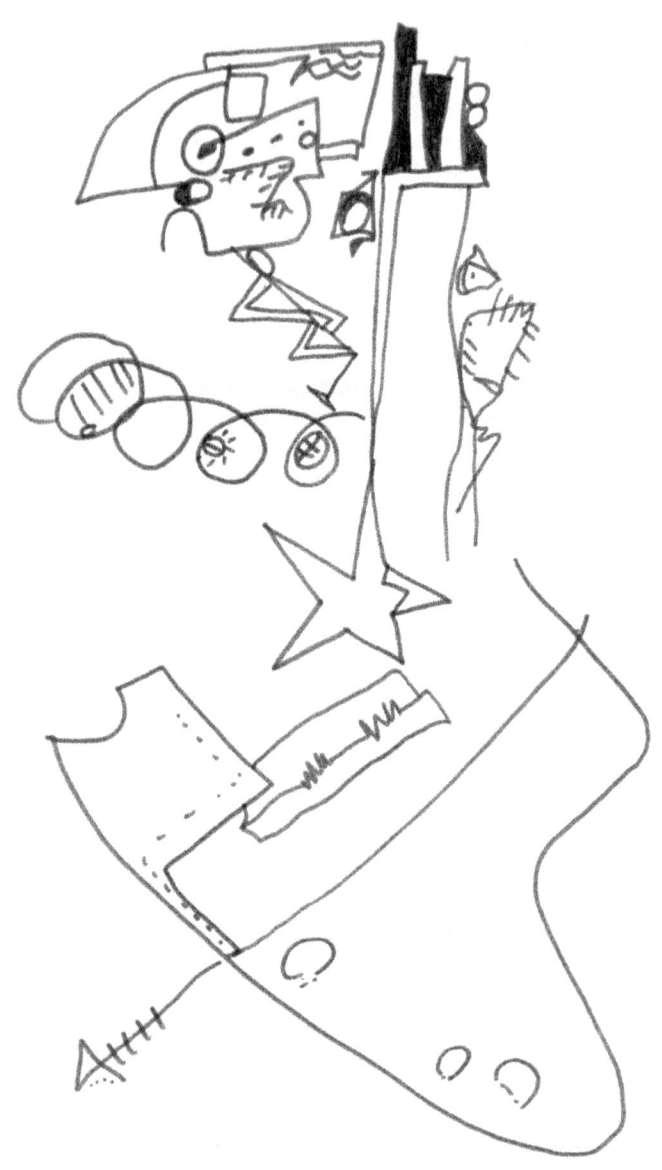

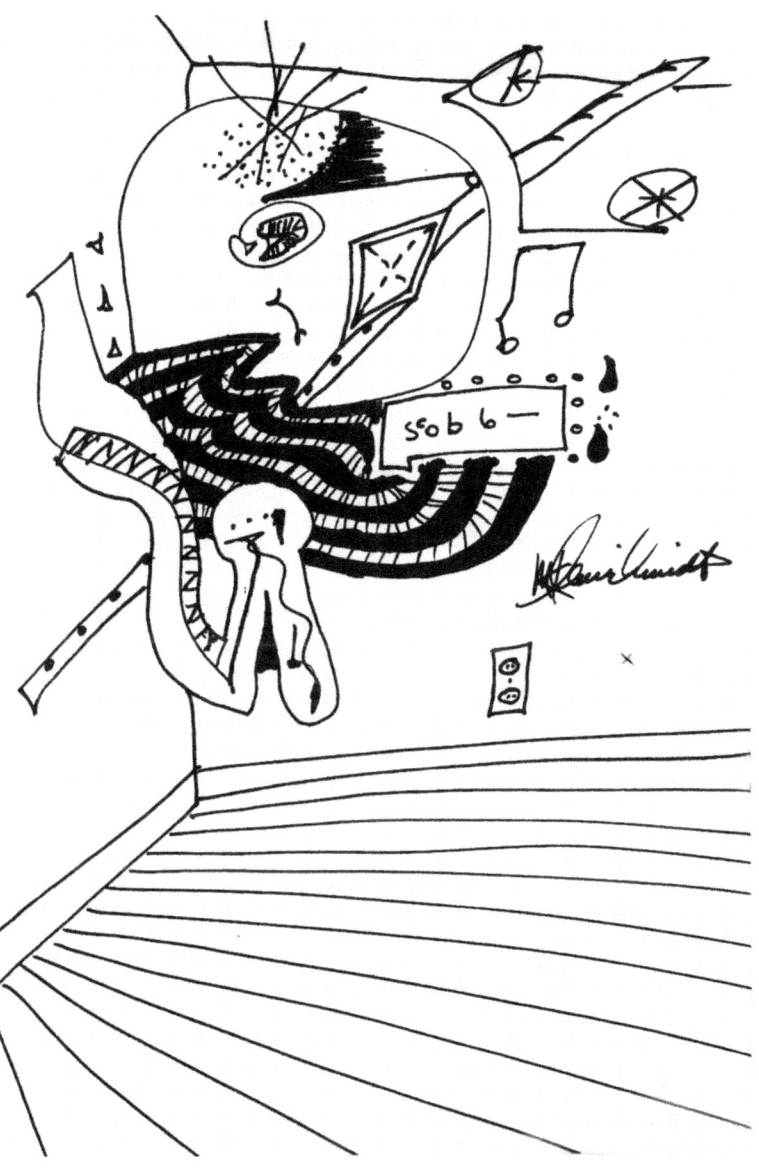

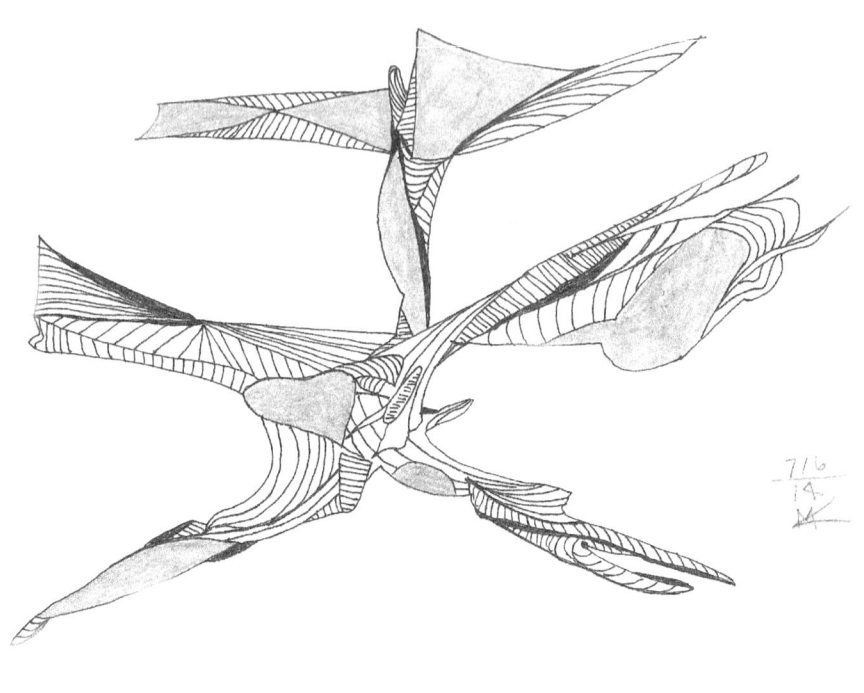

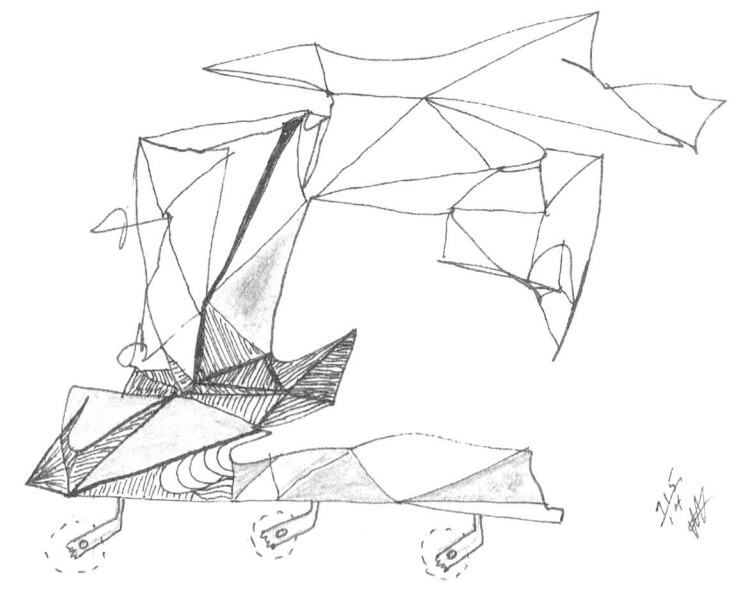

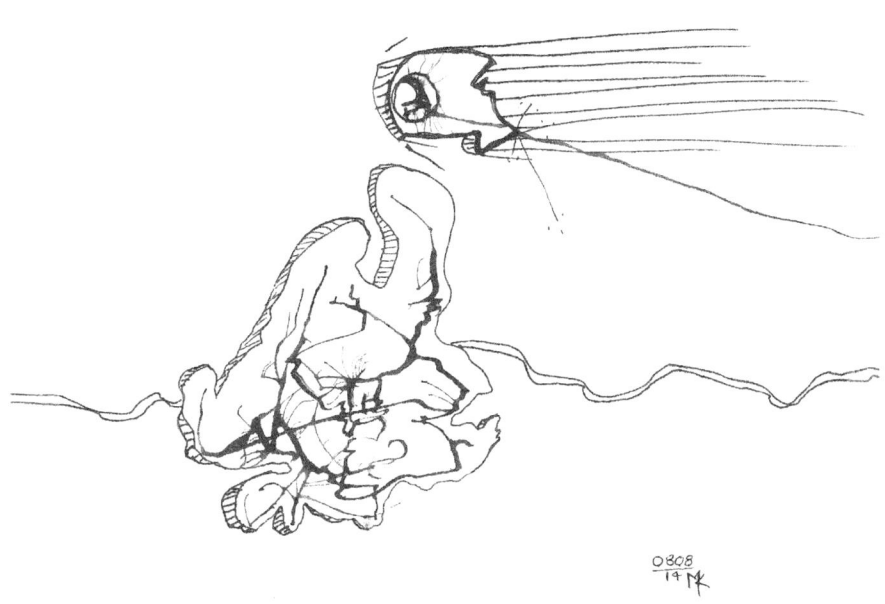

0808
19 MK

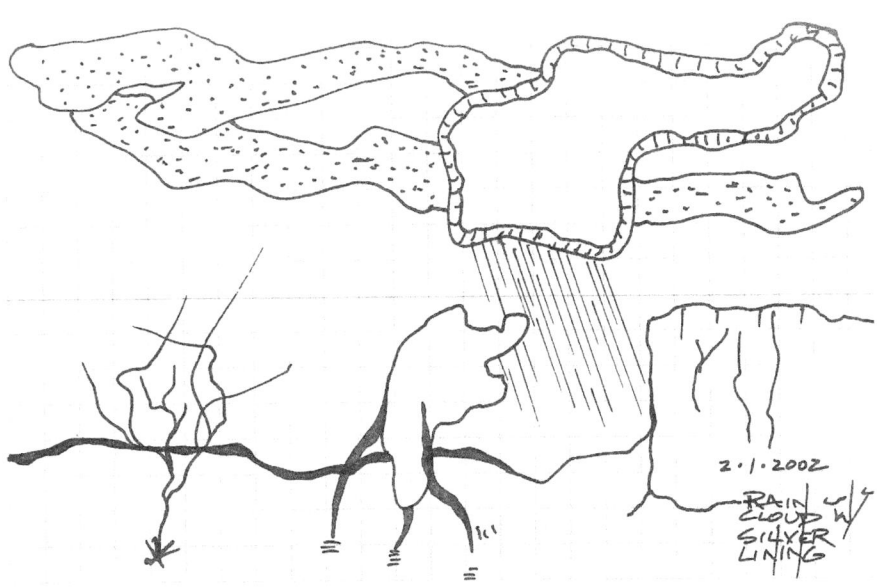

2.1.2002

RAIN w/
CLOUD w/
SILVER
LINING

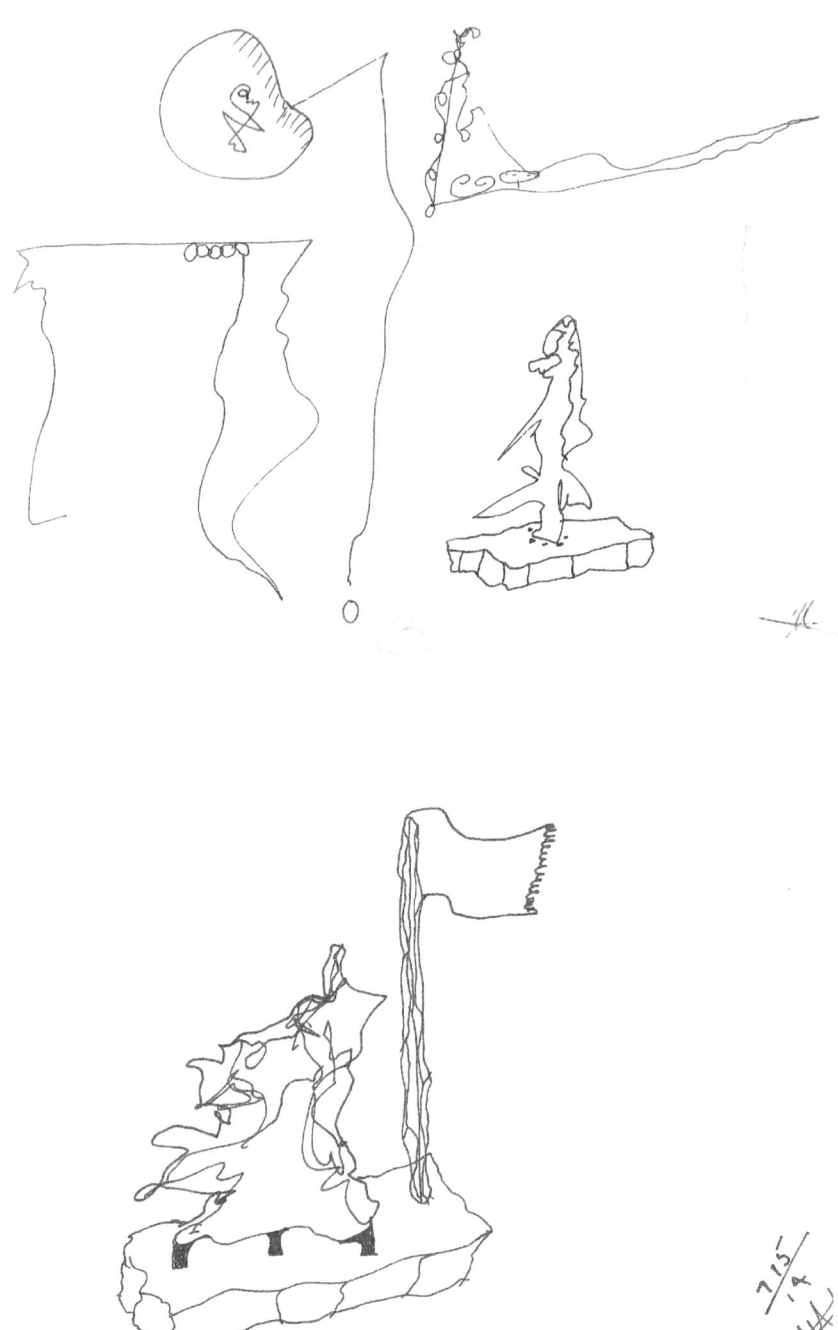

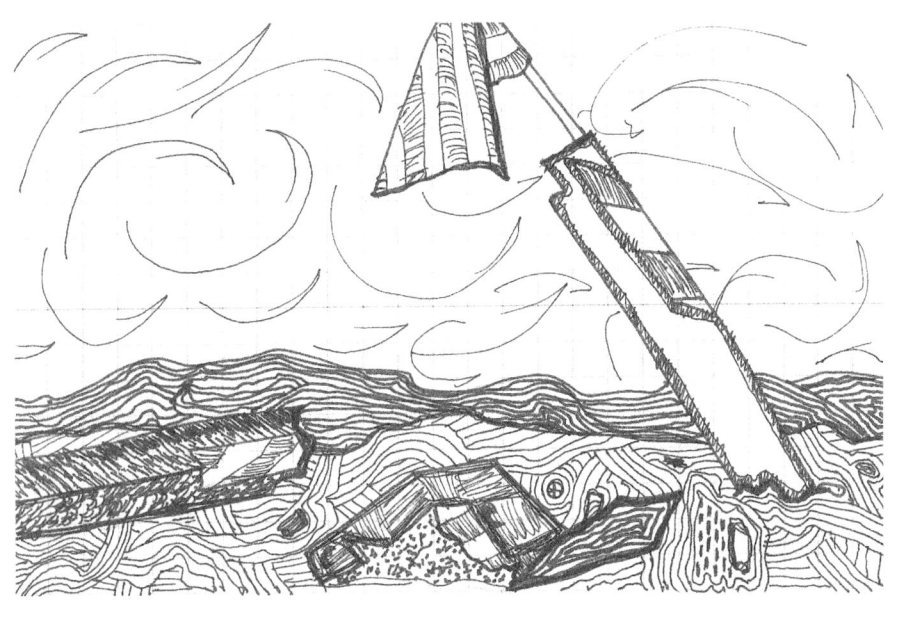

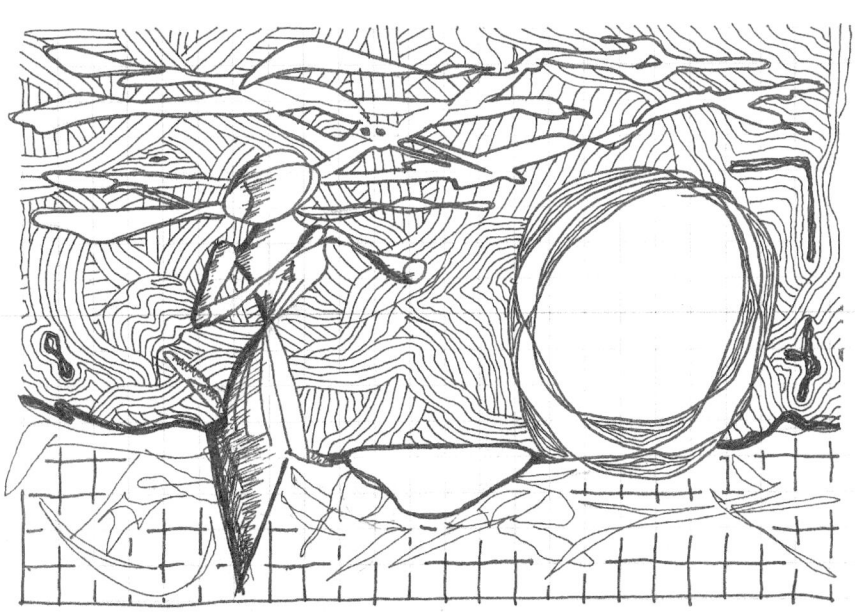

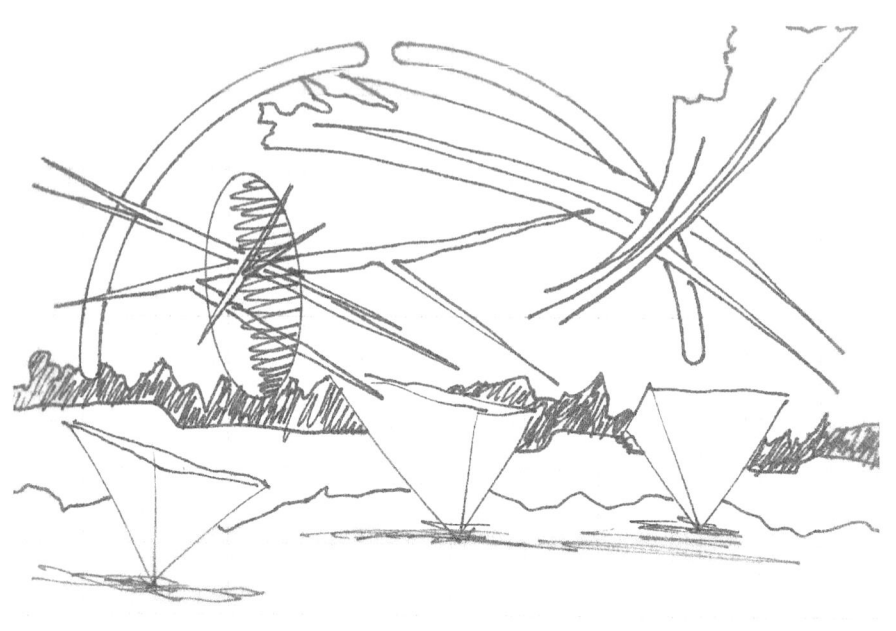

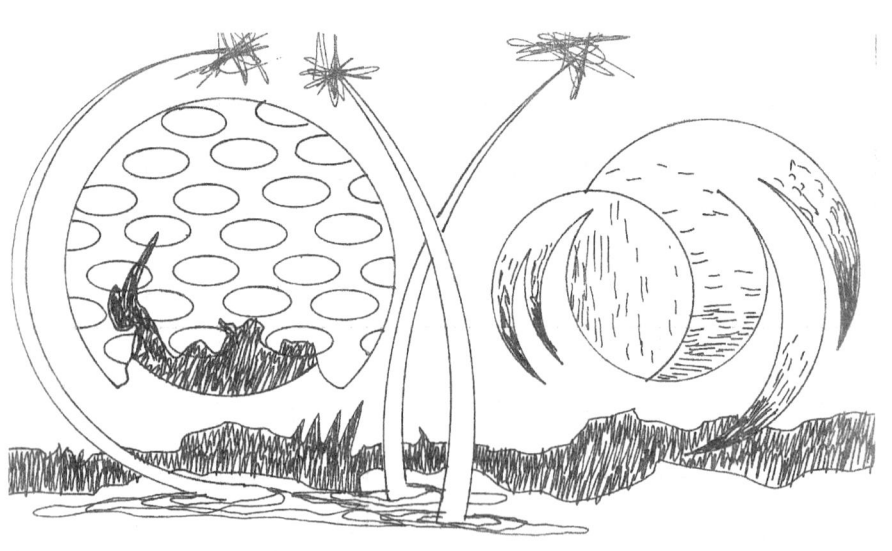

28·12·01

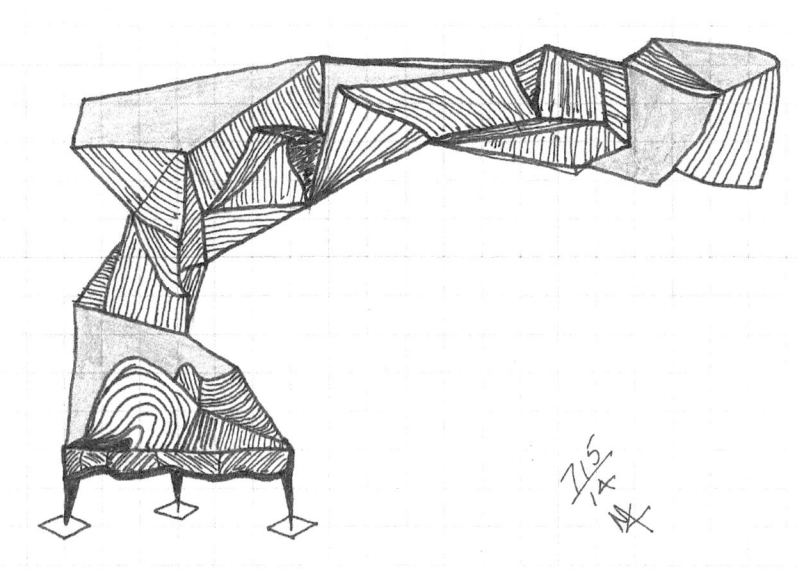

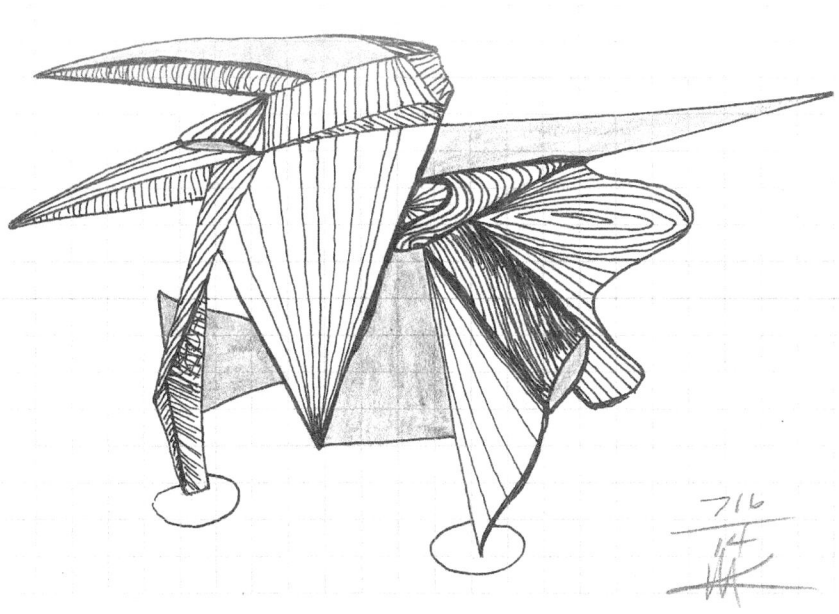

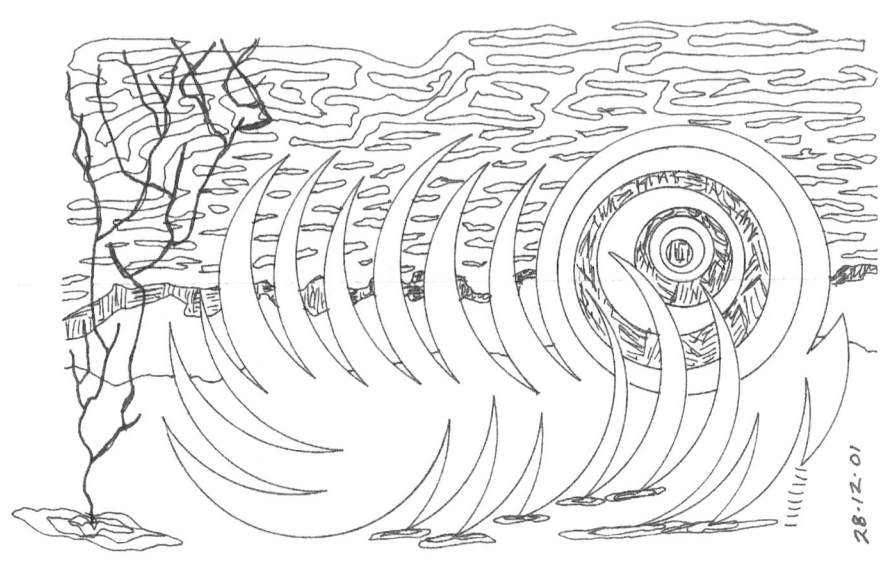

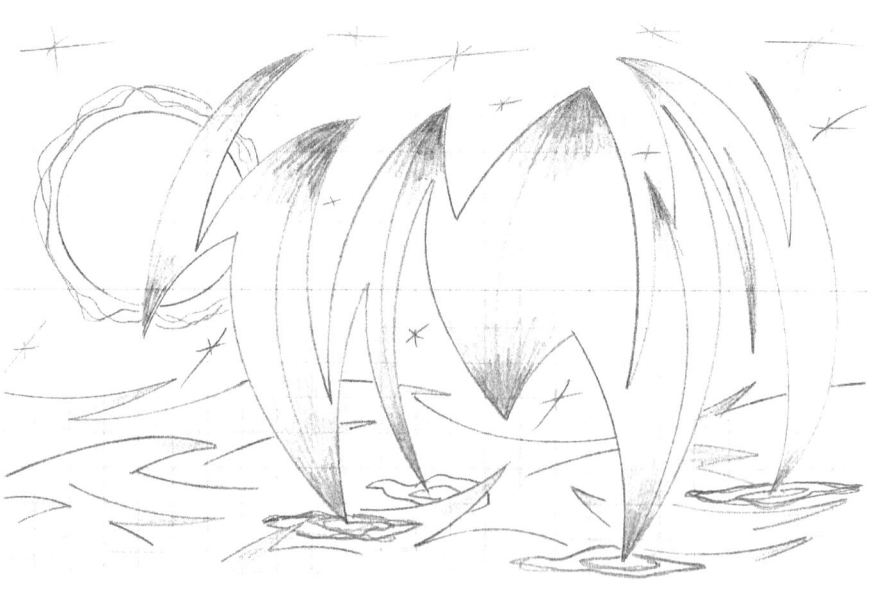

34

PAINTINGS

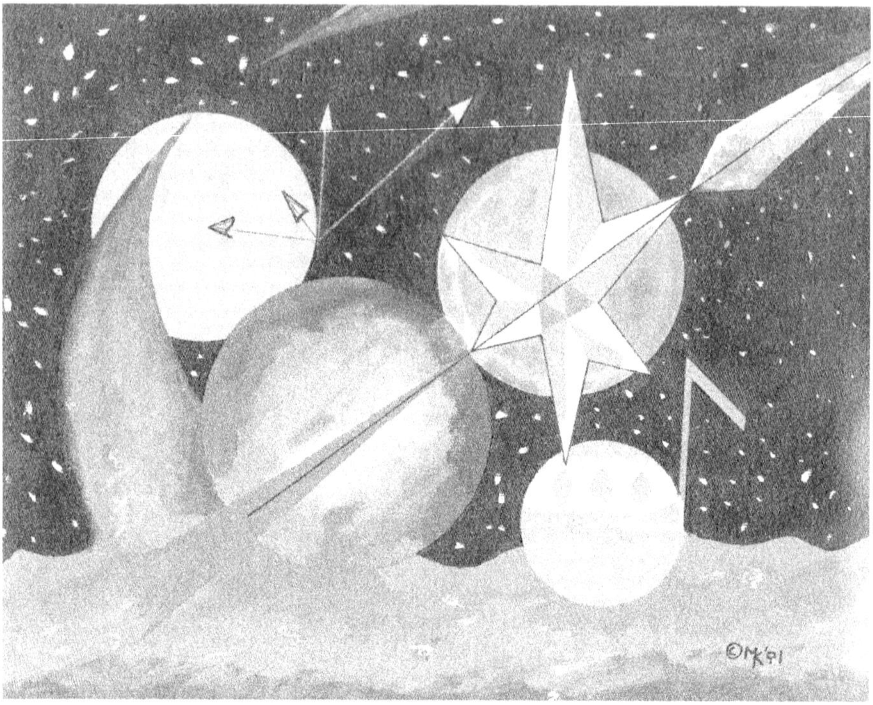

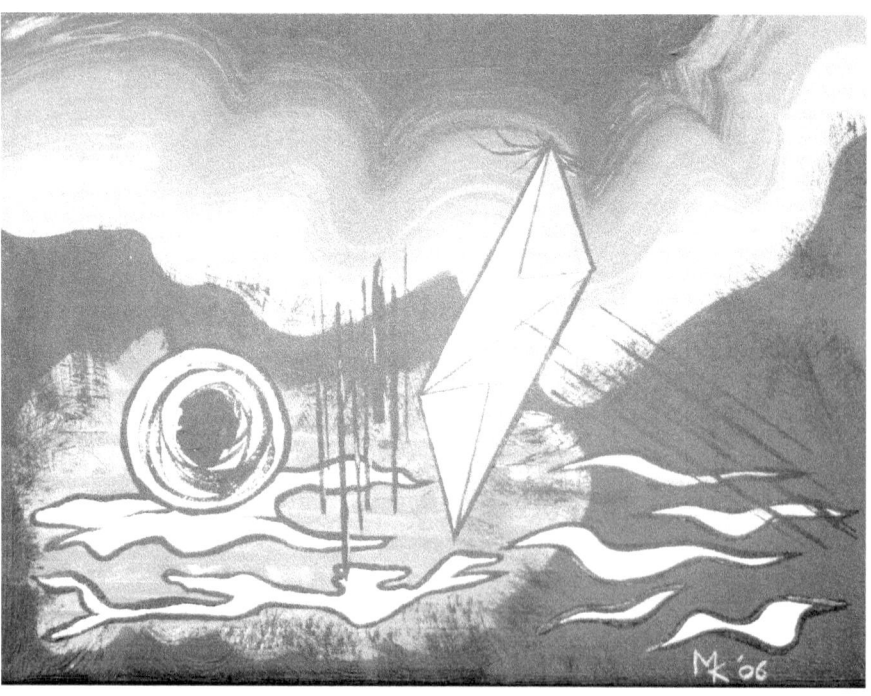

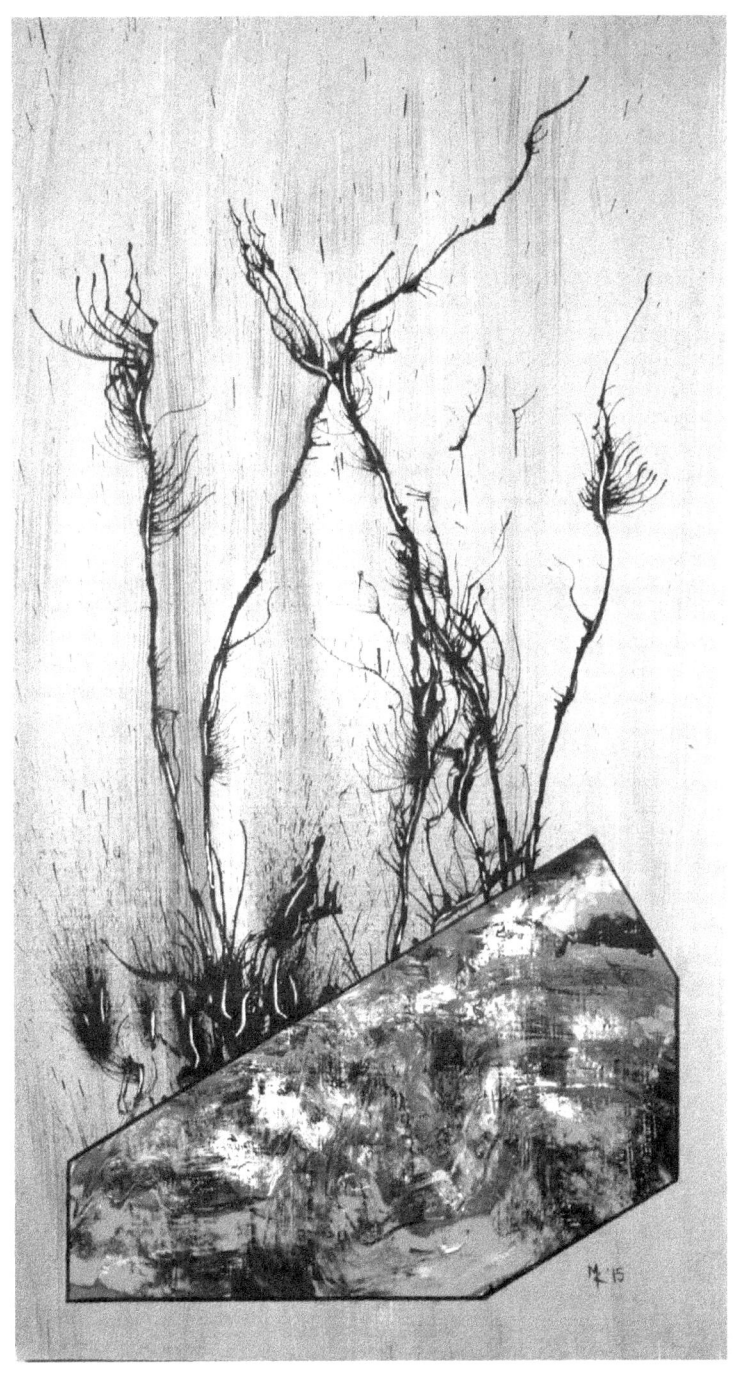

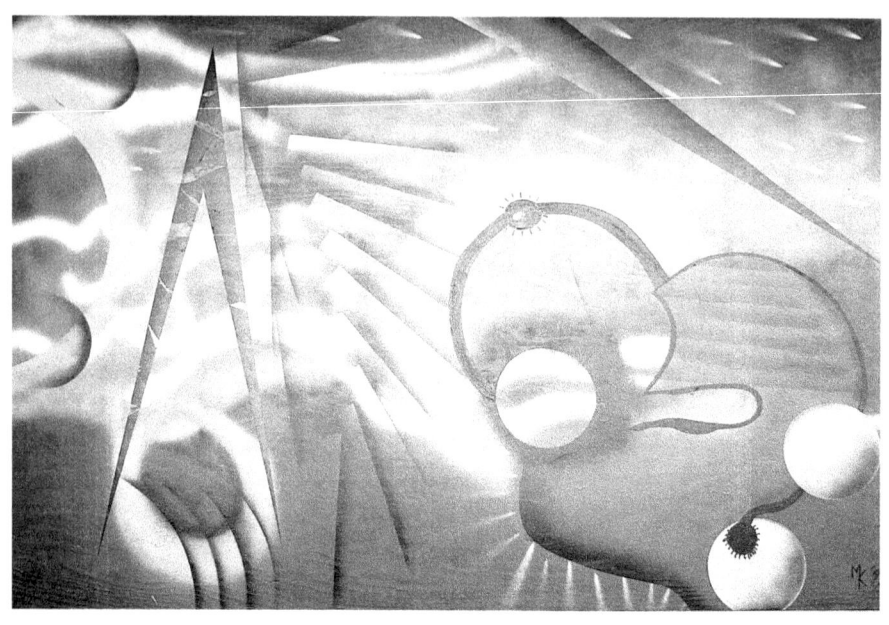

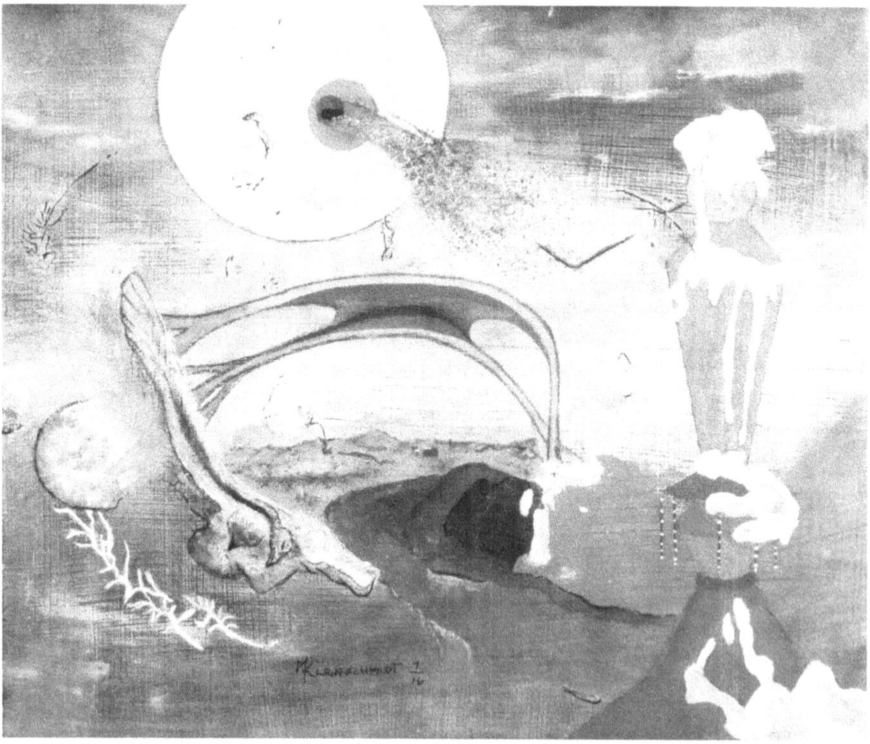

SCULPTURES

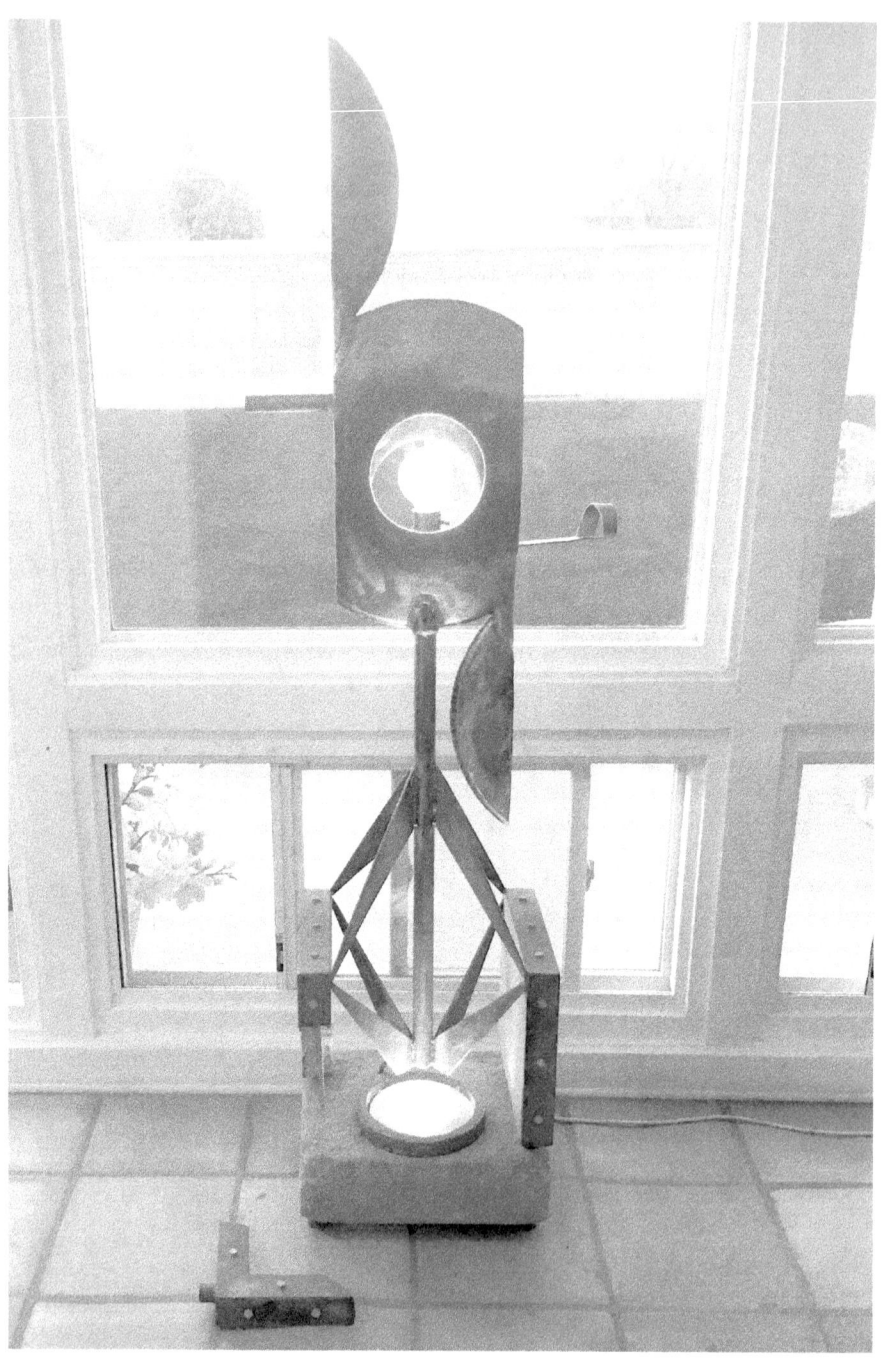

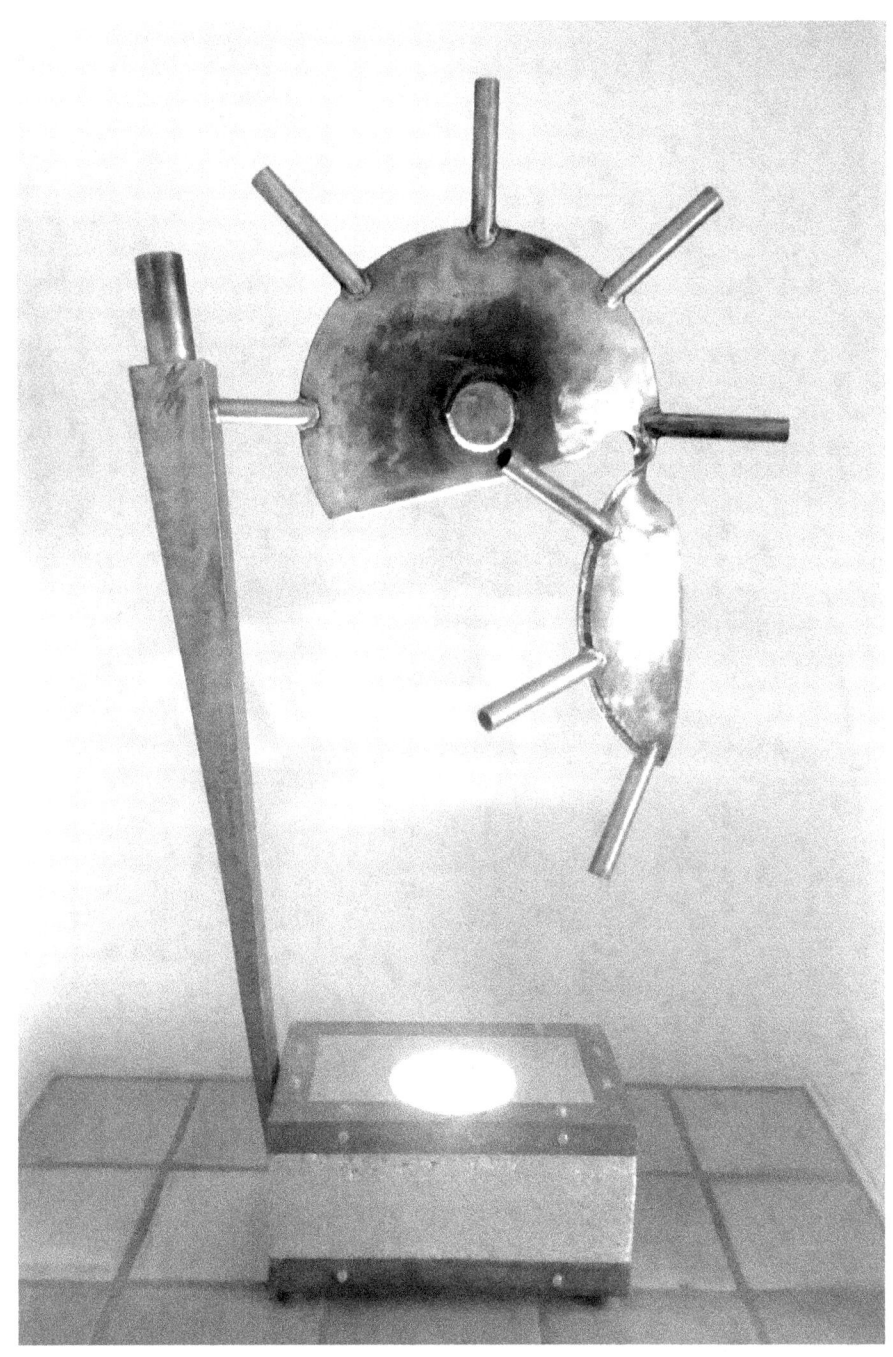

41

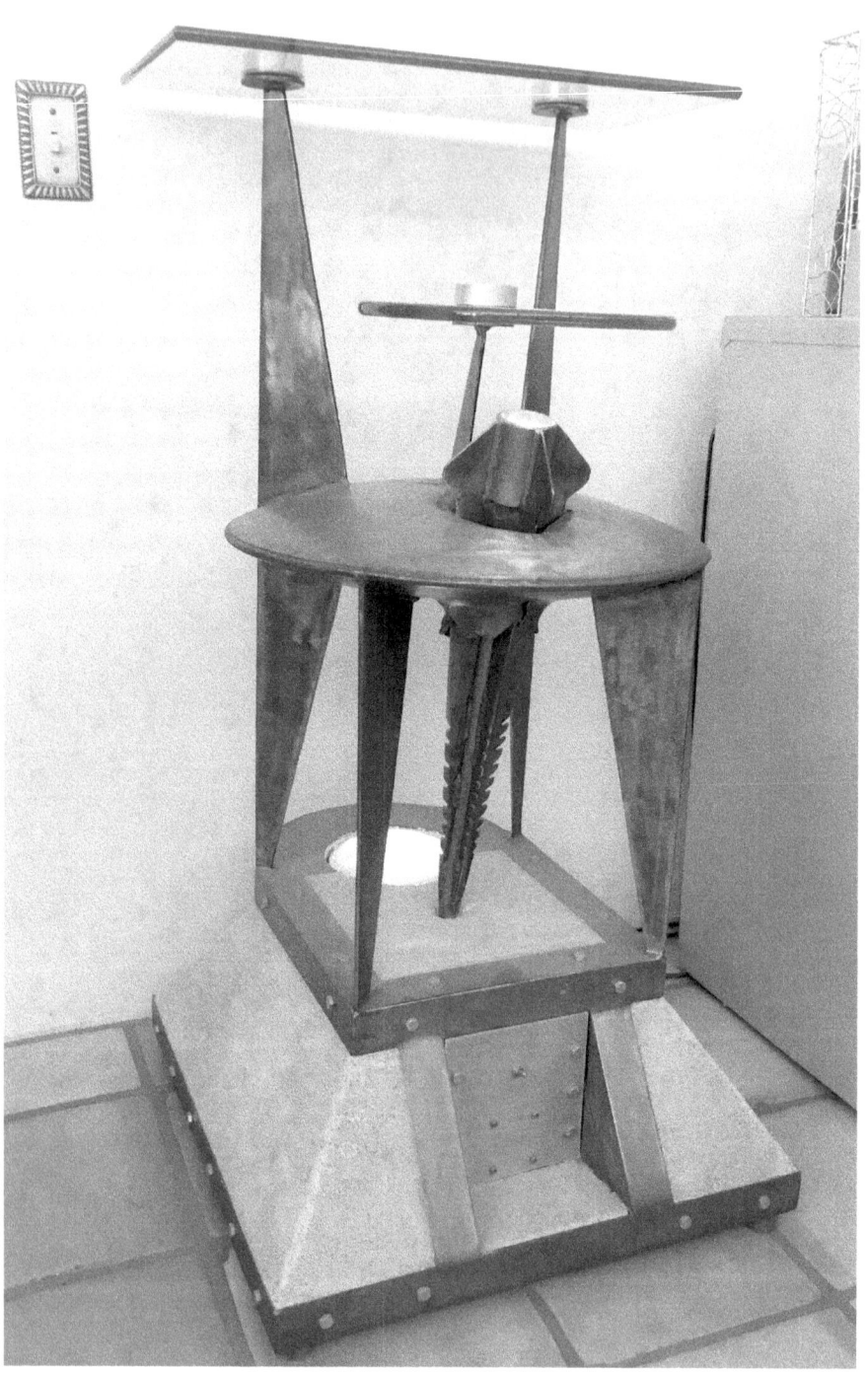

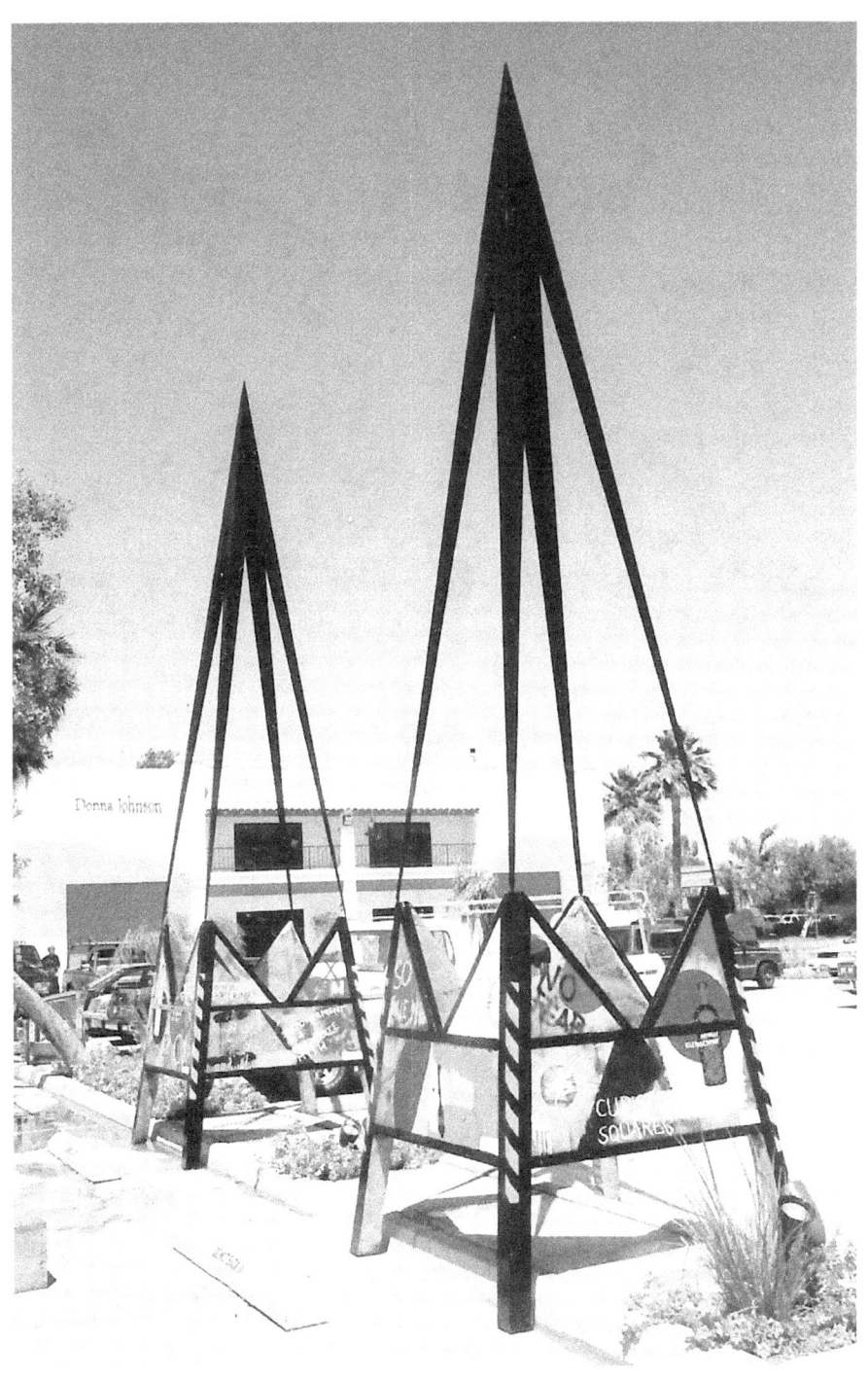

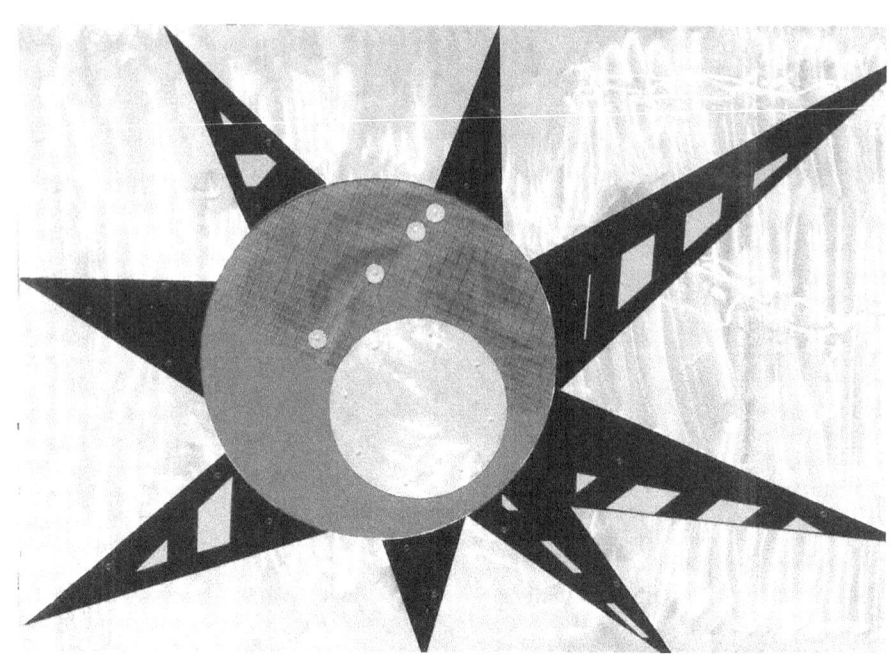

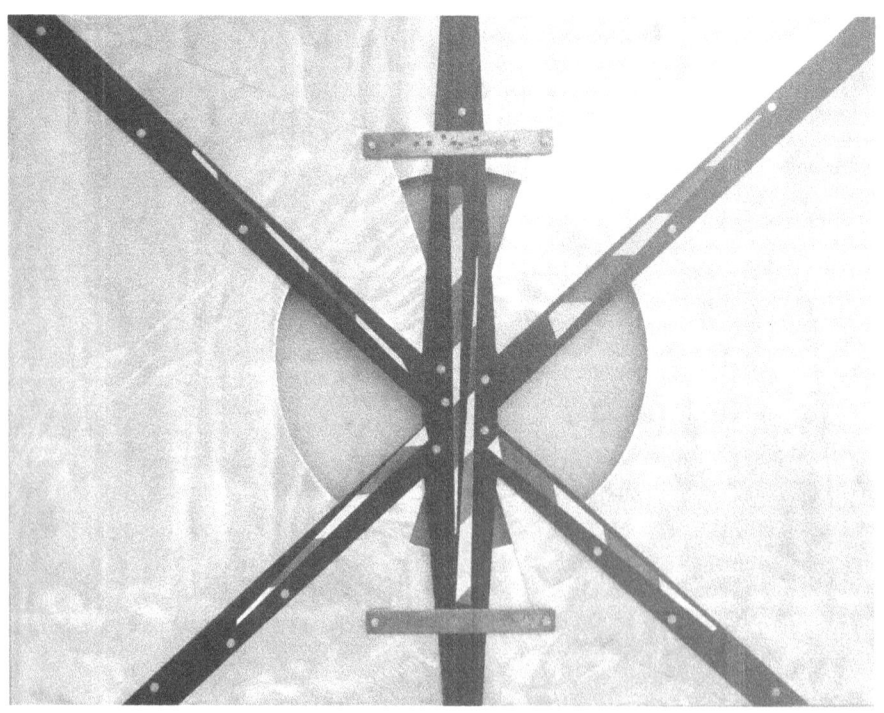

44

PROSE AND POETRY

An Interview with Dodee Elvia Dahting

M: When did you begin traveling alone?

DE: For the greater part of 40 years,
From the time when de hearto crystallized,
Through the melt mutation repertory,
Till when then began instantly and forever gone.

M: Really. If it was so much work, why did you
bother?

DE: Indeed the deed is mighty small,
Unless all no purpose at all but
To giggle and rangle for some solution,
To every moment a quiz, and
Solutionless is to lack confrontation.
Additionally, to a package of deciphering
Lingo must be located an application and,
Failing this, that is to fail tion,
Leaving an empty face filled with wholly naught.
And you know where that's at!

M: No, I don't.

DE: Here. It's there, and the only difference
Is none at all with it all.
I dare not talk about all with two parts,
Pair ever because a word doubled only contradicts
Itself, so also does the impression expressed.
Expressed, it dies
And mocks its own reason to be.
Fear of dying within lifetime,
For presenting the mock prototype singed,
As only it can see, consumed,
For lack of nothing
Is enough to freak anybody out.
Ain't that right, brother Mike?

M: So where do you go from here?

DE: Inside. (pause) Inside a nonessential view.
To hunt for a tickle, a trickle,
A scriggle, a lie to look between
The word double for some radiant
Bit of contradiction that can be excised and
Examined for the instant of its solo brilliance,
Until it too is compromised by a definition and
Resolves itself with the tarnish of two parts,
Paired, singed and consumed by admiration.

M: I'm sorry I asked.

DE: Don't worry about it.

The Corner

My mind when cornered is
A mind zapped from whatever
Connection was imagined of
What being alone would be
Like, tonight, over coffee.

Imagine real romance, a
Mind's eye view of
Walkers as they bounce or
Was that an image?

Imagination of tandem strollers
Is beyond the mind's eye
So I must be awake.
Good coffee.

Mine More

Mine more, more more,
Enough is never enough,
Enough good, enough greater good.
Men in black suits sit at desks in rooms
Attended by faithful disciples,
By hatchet men,
By assassins.

Development for a price.
Welcome to the first world.
Have some money.
We have money for you.
We will help you grow.
We will help you be like us.

Thunderdog

Seabird, what do you see from up there?
Can you see the sea?
Can anybody see the sea?

"Liberation from gravity by the wind,"
Says the seabird.
"Those are people down there.
See how they crowd the cliff's edge.
I wonder if those people are human.
The cliff gives me the wind.
The cliff gives people the edge of the sea,
The sea that I can see.

"For people the sea is death.
For humans the sea is a chance for life,
A liberation from gravity by the sea wind.

"Look, humans, see the sea?
Beware humans, the seductive sea.
Death is liberation too.
Rising on the wings of reality.

"Humans see the sea.
It's hard to ignore a mountain of water.
The mountain collapses in a thunderclap,
Leaving only a shadow,
An echo from a stone cliff,
A reflection.
Soon it too dies."

On a blue sea,
Whipped to snow-capped emerald mountains,
The seabird sits and stares.
Stares at a rubber mammal,
Another angel of gravity, riding on the sea wind.
Or it is a human?
Only time will tell.

RATTLESNAKE RUN

*Editor's Note: On May 31, 1984, Michael Kleinschmidt
embarked on a road trip from Los Angeles to Wisconsin
to "rescue" his nonrunning Volkswagen Beetle that his
mother wanted removed from her property. The following
is from recordings he made along the way as he drove a
Ford Falcon he came to call "The Rattlesnake." His audio
journal includes random reflections and notes to himself
for a book he planned to write at some future time, as well
as observations about the towns and people he came
across. Oddly, he doesn't mention the circumstances of
the Volkswagen; but his sister recalls he was unable to
get it running. In any event, the mission really was about
more than that.*

Good morning.

0515 hrs 31 May

You have to split off from the feeling of pain in order to
breath-hold dive.

Everybody wants to survive, and they all do it in their
own way the best they can.

It all has to do with reality and how much we radiate
a light. We radiate a light that is our light to be able to
see our own horizon. Without radiating a light, without
generating a light, we cannot see the horizon and we're
just blind to reality. It's not a matter of being blind, but
rather of not having any light. With photography, we
record what we see, and there's a whole interface with
light. But in the end, it's how well we can see our own
horizon and where that horizon is — how close it is, how
far away it is — and what kind of peripheral vision we
have of our horizon.

As a mechanic, when I see a broken light, my immediate
reaction is that I would like to fix it.

As a mechanic, you never lose a motor. You can always fix it. There isn't anything in this world that can't be repaired and made to work again — to make energy flow again. It's a mechanic's job is to keep the motor running, keep everything going, keep the light burning. Don't let the thing become inoperable.

Diving is accomplished out of sight of the horizon. You lose sight of the horizon when you make the dive. You hold your breath and you go to another world — a world where you're alien, a world without a horizon.

0735 hrs

Susan did not show up this morning. She was going to show up at seven and drop off the frog.

1300 hrs

She talks about how she's not going to screw up this relationship with Bruce, which started out by screwing up her relationship with me. She's so split off; she still believes she couldn't afford that place and that's the only reason.

She was supposed to be there this morning at seven o'clock to drop off the frog and wish me bon voyage. She didn't show. I drove past her house and her car was still sitting there. I'm not going to push any more issues with Susan.

A lost horizon doesn't mean an endless search for Shangri La. It means a simple coming to grips with being alive and being able to look at the world we project. We always have the option of moving. We're mobile, and we can build tools to change our projections. We have, through our learning and our skills, a vocabulary of being able to change and move and see where to move and how to change our realities.

The world that each individual lives in is that individual's own projection. It is sacred and cannot be manipulated by others unless we ... No! I can't be manipulated, period.

Internalizing reality rather than projecting reality makes people sick.

The toolmaker's job is to make a tool that makes somebody's life easier. And with his tool and his cleverness, he will always build a more complicated tool than the tools he used to build it — until, of course, so many tools are built that the tools then go looking for people, rather than people looking for tools. In all my vocabulary of how to do things, I was unable to penetrate Susan's armor. It takes a lot of armor to close somebody up inside.

Only people can project power into objects. And any one person can only project the power into the object that has power over the person. It is not put in by somebody else. You cannot transfer power in that way.

1900 hrs

Susan was blinded to a whole lot of unpleasant things about her by her laser beam of sexual energy. That hit my very small vulnerable spot and blinded me — just totally overwhelmed me. And in my projection of her, I couldn't see any of the snarling self-righteousness. It was all put aside. All my strong instincts were shackled.

0545 hrs 1 June

Hollywood on a misty gray dawn from the Hollywood freeway. It looks like a real hard-ass industrial town but with palm trees.

Near Exposition Boulevard, the overpasses and all the concrete have pictures of Latinos in murals painted on them. They're looking at everybody on the freeway like angry gods about to take their revenge.

This morning when I went over to visit Mary, to pick up the letter, she was all glassy-eyed and happy to see me.

If I can't touch it, I don't believe it. I like to be able to touch each picture in some way. It confirms that, yeah, it came from a particular place, as opposed to something that's electronic that has images but you don't have anything that you can really touch. It's just light bouncing around.

It's June 2 — a Saturday.

If the roads haven't been maintained, you are at the mercy of the people who made those roads. If you assume you're going to make your own roads everywhere, then you can never get tripped up. You can never get stuck.

There are some real dangers, some super hazards, of hooking into somebody else's dream — hazards not only for the individuals, but also for the human species as a whole.

I received a notice that my assigned risk auto insurance was going to cost more than what it was quoted, which was $500 a year — the minimum liability, no collision or anything on this piece-of-shit car.

A mechanic knows that if something is dented or crimped, you can straighten it. It may not be pretty, but it may be functional. The only person that can fix people is the person doing self-mechanic work. And that's what jumping into the abyss is all about. It's taking charge and being a mechanic on yourself.

0615 hrs 4 June

On the Mulholland exit off the San Diego freeway, getting onto Sepulveda Boulevard. My car is the ship for the traveler. Los Angeles has ships of illusion, delusion, and enlightenment and all kinds of other ships.

With Susan, there was no magic. She just taught me that I am vulnerable to somebody else.

When a person is traveling in the abyss, inside, there are no shortcuts. It's a hard, rough road.

0630 hrs 5 June

Splitting off is the sort of thing that actors have to be able to do. They have to not be themselves and be somebody else. I want to be able to have the feelings that I felt for Susan but not be so needy for it that I get hooked into a lie to achieve it. It's the part that goes with being vulnerable.

0615 hrs 6 June

It takes energy to build the structure so that energy can be dissipated efficiently. From concept to completion, building the structure is much more enormous than the energy that the structure contains.

0615 7 June

We are evolutionized beasts — no better and no worse than any other beast, except that we are able to conceptualize. Just the notion that we can think of ourselves as being better than others that think is what sets us apart. That's the difference between humans and everything else. It isn't will; it's ego.

When thinking in terms of the big picture, why build evolutionary structures? They don't just happen. Energy happens. Matter happens. But to push it into structure does not just happen. Life is not an accident. The answer to all these questions is not in the exterior world. Because if we are evolutionary beasts, we carry with us the codes of all the beasts before us. We are a composite of everything, plus the nuances that we are able to put in ourselves. So inside of us is where the answers are. The pathways are interior. The mind and body are the conceptual and emotional pathways to ego and the understanding and examination of ego. That's our bond to immortality. Ego is not structure. Structure bears ego.

Humans have a social need to contribute or compete. But that is not part of the journey. The journey is interior — into the abyss.

It's ego that gets us screwed up in terms of repressing our life will or life forces — ego that motivates us to go on the search.

How much water does it take to keep Palos Verdes green?

Drivers in Los Angeles like to stop right in the middle of intersections to make left-hand turns across traffic. They like to stop with their nose in oncoming traffic. Or coming out of driveways, they stop with their nose in the traffic.

Got the last of the big bugs out of the car at the smog place.

The fact that we can assign human attributes to animal behavior means that there is something about us that's different from animal behavior.

When we die, reality stops. The only shot that we have at learning anything is during life. That's the reason for the structure of everything — the *really* big picture.

How much energy is a person to put into something? As much as it takes. But how much does a particular project take? Energy management through a better feeling for structure. Entropy flows one way. Energy will always determine its own structure.

The scientist's view is limited, and one of the big problems is the observer's impact on what is being observed. Take a mechanistic view of figuring out how things work.

The whole projection is conjured up by something to learn. Its reality is our reality in another dimension. It has nothing to do with science. It has to do with mechanics, engineering, how things work. The mechanic's view, the explorer's view as opposed to the scientist's view, is the idea of just taking a look, as opposed to working out a hypothesis.

The mechanic's view is that there is nothing that can't be built or can't be fixed. It's just a matter of energy. You'll never get a tool to do more than what it took to make the tool. However, if you make ever-more sophisticated tools with less-sophisticated equipment plus energy, it's not, as it might seem, anti-entropic. It's not because it takes the energy to make the thing that you will never get out of it. That would mean working with the simplest tools is the most efficient way to operate as a mechanic.

It's impossible to have a standardized reality when the observer affects what is being observed. It's a projected reality.

Thunderdog is the analogy to keeping calm when diving. Don't panic in a highly energetic situation. The thunderdog experience of keeping one's shit together, trying to accomplish something like finding the answer when everything is coming unglued around you. Not just surviving, but surviving with grace under pressure.

Part of the search is to do, initially, a lot of small things and develop the vocabulary quickly and without a lot of commitment to one particular approach, any one particular concept, any one particular emotion, any one particular skill. But just turn out a lot of little stuff — all of it good stuff, all of it part of the search.

Joann, admittedly on her part, used every bit of skill that she had to repress my energy, because she was so threatened by me as a powerful person. And I'm still recovering from that.

Before 1970, I had the fire I'm beginning to feel now. Again! Finally! There are plenty of followers in this world, but there are very few people able to figure things out for themselves. Like when Elona says she and Tom want to help. Help my ass. How about her and Tom figuring out how to do their own shit?

I don't want to lead a bunch of followers, to help people find their way. Because what's important is the search for your own way — not that people follow a leader or that people lead followers. That builds up all kinds of problems.

Having to tape-record journal notes and take journal notes to remember what was said and then having John remark, "Can't you just remember or can't you think this out for yourself?" Even an eclectic scientist has a very narrow, tunnel-vision view and a specific style of thinking, whereas the journalist is exposed to all styles of thinking and reports on what he observes, and the notes are his data. The journalist is far more eclectic than a scientist. Journalists interview scientists; scientists don't interview journalists. The journalist is interested in what the scientist knows, what the politician knows, what the educator knows. But none of these people are interested in everything the journalist knows.

The city of Los Angeles is made up of left-hand turns across traffic.

You're a lucky person if you get what you pay for. That's especially true in manufactured goods. With raw material, you generally get what you pay for; but in manufactured goods, there is no way to know if you are getting good value unless you watched it being put together. So a good way to get what you pay for is to manufacture it yourself from raw materials.

The artist follows his internal flow, but the mechanic manages structure and energy. So it's the mechanic that says, "In so much space, you can work in such and such a scale and be able to work in such and such a space. You can get wacko with your scale and it will never work. It just won't. It will be too much energy input and not enough return to the structure."

2327 hrs 8 June

On Buena Vista, about to get onto the Ventura Freeway heading for Las Vegas. We are on the road again.

This morning was the first time I could get the car up to 55 miles per hour without it sounding like it was going to come unglued.

It's about an hour into this leg of the trip and I'm already starting to zonk out and have hallucinations. Michael, don't go to sleep on me in the middle of the

60

I-10/I-15 interchange just because you have hallucinations of Chevys crossways in the road in front of you.

The car runs good at 45 miles per hour. It's going to be a long trip. I bought a pair of used tires and everything for it.

0445 hrs 9 June

Stopped at a little off-ramp, changed my blue jeans, and fell asleep for three hours.

Because of the nickity-nick in the engine, my style of driving is a bit weird. I can step on the gas going up a hill and get up to 55 and 60. But going down the hill, I have to stay 45 or under to keep the piston from slapping.

Going into the orange glow just before sunrise with Jean-Michel Jarre's "Oxygène" playing in the background and the overpass and the little-bitty mountain off to the side of it. The sun is going to come up right on the road. It's real eerie. The colors run from hot orange to a lime green glow to turquoise. The first sun peeks out from behind a tree with a telephone pole and wires running across the top of the scene. The road curves right in front of a half sun on the horizon. As I blink my eyes, streaks from the sun move toward me and away from me. And all the time cars are passing me. The sun is right on the horizon, and the car in front of me is driving in a pool of light. His wheels are driving in a pool of orange light, with streaks blasting past him as I blink my eyes. The sun streaks on the road have me blinded. Cars kind of float by my port side. One after the other they slip by and disappear into the light.

The exit ramp and the silhouetted stop sign launch right into the sun — into the sun streaks.

"Dignity is valuable, but our lives are valuable too." — David Bowie.

The road is like a little ski jump. You go up the hill and it looks like you are going to jump.

I think that part of my drowsiness at the wheel has got to do with engine fumes. So I've got all the windows open and I feel much more awake.

"I've got to find a passage back to the place I was before." — The Eagles.

I kick the car into neutral on the downslopes.

Just passed a correctional institution. Part of the trend in correctional facilities is to turn the prisons over to private, commercial enterprises. What's the next thing? Is it going to be private enterprise picking up the policing? And how about private enterprise picking up the judging and people who haven't been elected doing the legislation?

I said I was going to be in Las Vegas at 10 o'clock. Here it is 10 o'clock and I'm rolling through town. In fact, I'm going to get on the off-ramp in about one minute and it's about one mile away.

I think it's all the atomic testing and nuclear radiation that makes people so security conscious in Las Vegas.

1100 hrs

There are four baseball diamonds behind the city college. This is the Chianne Sports Complex Department of Parks and Recreation. Beautiful baseball diamonds. A woman's softball league is playing — women with thick legs having an all-American good time. Little did they know that a stone-cold free thinker, a warm-blooded free thinker was walking right through their midst, hair standing on end as a pair of fighter jets are coming in for a landing.

At 1115 hrs, I called Maggie from the 7-Eleven phone. A guy answered and said, "She's at work. She's working until 5." So the decision to be made is to hang around and wait until 5 o'clock and try and get hold of her and go out this evening or cut loose, give it another shot another time and get on my way. Well, seeing as how I like managing energy in effective and efficient ways, I'll throw a tank of gas into the car, check the tires, and hit the road. How much energy am I willing to put into something? And with my recent experience with women, I'd just as soon drive than sit around and wait.

Should I go to Salt Lake City or Colorado? Or should I do both?

To Salt Lake City. It's nine hours and worth every minute to run on up there and check it out on a Saturday night.

Joann was always so self-assured about everything. Every move, every statement was intimidating and straightforward. She used it to her maximum leverage on this artist boy from the middle of Wisconsin. I wasn't any match for her. I wasn't in her league in terms of skills for manipulating people and the incentive to manipulate people. I just like doing my stuff, period.

Bought fireworks for Charlie from an Indian roadside stand. The whole Indian family was behind the counter. They were selling their fireworks in this little two-by-four stand.

The car runs 50 miles per hour all day long, except when I get to hills; then it's 45 mph down the hill. Going up the hill, I can run it at 80 mph and the engine doesn't rattle; but going down, it rattles at 45 mph.

Sitting in the car watching the hood munch up the road. It's like I'm projecting a reality that I'm devouring.

Littlefield, Arizona. A girl sitting outside the gas station. Of course they have beer for sale.

Drew a picture of the old woman staring at me when I started my car and it rattled. Rattle, rattle, rattle. I'll call the car Rattlesnake. That's what this is: The Rattlesnake Run.

The energy stored in a structure is only the potential of the structure collapsing — the energy given off as the roof collapses to the floor.

The Rattlesnake Run is an example of getting the job done in a limited-resource manner — that of thunder-dogs.

When Joann met me, I was on fire inside, walking in all kinds of uncharted turf — a lot of places where there was unsure footing. She did everything she could to knock me off balance, and she did.

The thing I like about little towns is their Laundromats are all clean and spiffy. Everybody has a lot of respect for the Laundromat, because that's where they do their laundry.

It's weird the number of cars that are broken down on the road. It makes me really nervous.

All the cars break down — except for the survival wagons. They are the ones that run and run and run and don't get stolen and don't get screwed up, because they're already screwed up.

64

You can't travel in your own projection, because it's like going to the movies. But you can learn from it. You can get clues on where to look inside. What you're doing is seeing what's inside projected out. And what it does is it tells you where to go on your inward journey. You can project outward, but you can only travel inward. And your reality is the data that you have to set up your roadmap — to chart your course inside.

Filmore, Utah. Stopped at the grocery store and there were two women and six kids all just carrying on and being women and kids. I'm walking into the store, this little country store, my hair standing on end like it always is and there's an old man, a happy old man, and a guy 30 years old, overweight and aggie looking, but jolly. And the old man approaches me and says, "Pardon me, stranger, will you hit this guy for me?" And they both break out laughing as I just wander through.

There's nothing rational about a subatomic world that behaves irrationally. Everything is crazy. But how crazy is crazy? How big is big? How small is small? How irrational is irrational? What are the limits? That's what I'm about: expanding those horizons, pushing them back further and further and further. Look over the horizon. Look under the horizon. Look around the horizon. Chase it. Follow it. Push it.

Levan, Utah. What a cute little town.

There's no way to eliminate boundaries, but how far back can we push them? How skillful can we become to create empires with boundaries so vast that they are empires of reality? Just rich, full, and lush.

It might be my imagination, but The Rattlesnake might be nicking less and less.

Always come into Salt Lake City at sunset.

This is the middle of June and it's cold and snowy. The air is so clear up here that coming into Salt Lake City at night, it just sparkled. Most of the cities are on the alluvial fans of the mountains, so they are kind of like little amphitheater seats and you can see the whole city, all the lights. It's just like you are flying in, coming in for a landing at a low altitude.

I like the shadows' interplay. A car was just on an on-ramp and tried to squeeze … Let's see, I was in the right-hand lane and the car was on the on-ramp and he was going to try and pass me but then decided not to so fell back and then went around in back of me to my left-hand side. While he's doing this, all the shadows of the car are kind of scraping around, moving around the car as I'm going forward and he's going in back of me with his lights.

Utah State Pen is right next to the freeway. Driving past at night, boy is the thing lit up. It would make a great photograph.

This is the town to come and party. In that country-western bar, there were two women for every man, and there was not a dog in the bunch. They were all very friendly. It looked like a good band, a good dance band, country-western, all about 35 years old wearing base-ball hats. Except the drummer wore a giant cowboy hat and sunglasses.

Everybody in the bar was wearing cowboy boots, cowboy shirts, blue jeans, fancy belts. The men had nice, trim beards. Their hair was combed nicely. The women had their hair done nice. They were wearing cowboy boots or high-heeled shoes with blue jeans and tight shirts.

The band was playing and the place was packed and jammin'. I walk in and I'm sitting at the bar with my hair standing on end, with my bomber jacket, off on another planet, checking it all out like I invented the whole thing and there it is. Girls at the pool table. Wow, to have been there three hours earlier and gotten dibs on the pool table would have been more than a person could possibly bear. I should just come here and live. This town knows how to party.

The giveaway was a sign that said, "The Nome Lounge" that had a big Coors sign in the window. I gotta get a damn cowboy hat and some boots and a pickup truck. There's also a bunch of bikers. Gosh, what an interesting town this is.

I almost missed the I-80 East connection. I made a typical California-cross-the-median-through-blackberry-brambles, off the ground, just to make the exit ramp from four lanes over.

0700 10 June

In a view area on a hill just outside of Salt Lake City. Spent the night curled up in the front seat. The Rattlesnake sitting among a flatbed, camper, two motor homes, a pickup with a camper shell, and a car with a rental trailer on it. Surrounded by mountains, about 1,000 feet below the snow line. And the road up the hill is snaking past us. A wooly-headed truck driver is checking his tires, his oil. Kicks the tire. Good morning.

The sky is an iridescent blue in places, with clouds hanging down almost to the mountaintops. It looks real stormy.

I should get a new set of sparkplugs.

Picture snaking up this lonely mountain with word balloons of music and ocean swells coming out of it. The road leads into clouds with streaks coming out of them.

Trying to pour a cup of coffee. Going down a hill in The Rockies. Going down this hill means business, but you have got to pour a cup of coffee.

The Top-Siders I'm wearing just don't fit in cowboy bars.

The car going down the road with a word balloon: "Is this the road to nowhere? Am I there yet?"

Where is nowhere? I'm looking for a place called nowhere.

Wyoming State Hospital in Evanston.

Fireworks are legal in Utah and Wyoming, but Wyoming I've seen has got the really hot fireworks stores next to the I-80.

Something to consider is the master/apprentice relationship. A lot of times, that tradeoff is worth it, because if a thunderdog has really got his act together, he should be able to absorb everything — take from the master all of his skills and apply them to his own reality, his own traveling, and his own search. So the winner really is the apprentice; and the loser is the master, because all he gets is structure for a minimal amount of energy. But what the follower gets is skills for his own reality.

Then, of course, dynasties are really sick. Manipulation of other people's energies — that's preying on faults and weaknesses in another person's character structure.

Holy headwinds!

People burn up energy for convenience more than anything else. Even me. This trip is totally unnecessary. But it's convenient.

This headwind is sure killing my gas mileage. There's a lot of shit in the air making my eyes really hurt. It affects my seeing. It affects my projection. There's dirt on the projector lens.

Little America between Evanston and Rock Springs, Wyoming, at mile marker 68, is in the middle of nowhere.

10 June

I keep telling everyone that I'm making this run to get my car and my tools. That's not true. I'm making the run to rediscover who I am and what my paths are.

It will be really hard going in and visiting at the TV station. Because the question will be, "What are you doing now and how are things going out there?" And I don't know what I'm doing now and how things are going out there.

Wyoming — talk about expanded horizons!

One prairie dog standing on its hind legs right next to the road. The other prairie dog in the wheel track, lying there with just its legs pointing up into the sky, with just its legs kicking. It had been hit and its legs worked but nothing else did. And the prairie dog alongside the road was watching and wondering what the heck happened.

The last frontier for everybody is the journey they take inside.

Wyoming isn't real big on its rest areas.

The trouble I was having in terms of gas mileage was the fact that I was climbing up to the Continental Divide.

We're on the backside now, and I can't get this thing to use gasoline no matter how much I want it to.

When we are traveling, it's interesting to realize how many things we do to entertain ourselves along the way. That's true of the internal journey too.

Well, I think I'll photograph for a while. Well, I think I'll talk into the tape recorder for a while. Well, I think I'll listen to Laurie Anderson for a while. Well, I think I'll pull over and sleep for a while.

On our internal journey, I'm sure we do things to entertain ourselves just to keep from being bored. Because a lot of times, especially when you're traveling nowhere, you're just covering turf — miles and miles of endless turf.

Whoa! It's windy up here on top of the world.

A motorcyclist is camped out under an overpass during a downpour.

"Loyalty is valuable, but our lives are valuable too." — David Bowie.

Wouldn't it be something if on this trip I gave up the '60s and joined the world of the '80s? That was the last time I had any fun. To repress the energy inside me, I've had to split off so hard and so far. Susan was just the last straw.

The thing about drawing from photographs is that no matter how cheesy the resolution of the photograph, the resolution of the drawings is always the same.

There are some places in nowhere that are extremely inhospitable. I would really hate to break down up here in all the wind and snow and nothingness of central

Wyoming. Every five miles they have signs that say, "Strong winds possible next 5 miles."

Rational thinking, logical thinking, intellectual thinking is narrow-minded and bounded thinking. You might as well take your head and tie it up in a bunch of ropes and a paper sack. Maybe I'll do some pictures of people who have their heads tied up in knots.

There's another killer hill outside of Laramie. First gear, 20 miles per hour. I can tell it's steep when I can smell my transmission burning up.

I need a bumper sticker that says, "I break for hallucinations." If that were the case, I'd never get anywhere.

The automatic transmission is sure taking a pounding on this trip.

At UMW, I was having the best time of my life, and I decided to go live with Joann instead. She had me so buffaloed into thinking there was something wrong with me. I didn't have the courage to tell her that I didn't want to be with her.

The vacuum-actuated shift on the car doesn't work at high altitudes, because it doesn't pull the differential in vacuum.

Poles alongside the road with Scotchlite dots on them. If there's a pole that goes between the headlights and that whole line of markers, it will send a shadow down the markers and look like landing lights at an airport as the shadow travels up the line of markers from my headlights.

It was an interesting scene at the restaurant at Little America. It might merit a drawing. Standing there waiting for somebody to give me coffee for my Thermos and this guy and I are talking for a bit about weather conditions up the line. And on the other side of the counter is a guy with his family — like my father, kind of heavy and wanting to know everything. He asked, "Well, how far did you come from today?" I was dumbfounded, because I couldn't quite remember. And then I said, "Uh, Salt Lake City." And he said, "Yeah, all that time on the road and you get a little dizzy after awhile." It's like I was the expert, me in a bomber jacket and the hair. All I've got is a little Falcon with a knockin' rod and a rattlesnake noise that I still haven't been able to figure out what it is. It can't be too horrible, because the car is still running good.

It's stormy, windy. Alone on the road somewhere between Wyoming and Nebraska.

At the rest area in Cheyenne, another traveler asked me where the next rest area was heading west and I reported to him that the rest-area situation is awfully grim. One traveler giving a report of what nowhere is like in that direction. It's just a courtesy between travelers.

All we can know is nothing about nothing. Because if we do something about nothing, it wouldn't be nothing anymore. It would be something.

Hitchhikers try to ride along on somebody else's reality — steeds of reality. They don't have a steed of reality of their own. Or if they do, it's not capable of making the trip. Or if it is capable, for whatever reason they have, they want to ride on somebody else's reality. It's "take what you can," but it's true that they do find somebody.

I'm beginning to hallucinate again. It's about 11 o'clock at night. It's raining. The windshield wipers are going. I keep thinking I see the heads of the Jackson Five in the road ahead of me, but they are really big.

72

A thin black octopus just swam away from my wind-shield.

I'm looking for a rest area. And until I find one, which I think is right ahead, I hope, I'm right smack dab in the middle of an electrical storm. Lucky me.

As I pulled into the rest area, it has started to hail. At least the rest area is on top of a hill. There's nothing like high ground during an electrical storm.

Hear that? It's like f'ing popcorn.

Between 0400 and 0430 a.m. 11 June

The Rattlesnake likes Nebraska.

For any traveler, journey preparations are delicate things. You have to take enough, but not too much. It's like preparing for an ocean voyage. Redundant systems are nice if you have the room to take them with you. If you're just going out diving in heavy surf, you can't take a lot, because everything you take becomes a liability as well. It's the same with being on the road.

Journeys don't have any destinations, but they do have direction. I like to keep the direction a solid nowhere.

The grounding is the packaging of this. It's not a matter of ego, pride, business, or any of that stuff. It's a matter of grounding. Traveling in nowhereland is great, but you need a sort of grounding. Otherwise, you can get lost. There are a lot of travelers who are lost in nowhereland.

Surf is the introduction to nowhereland — a place that doesn't exist except for the energy. The same place at a low tide on a calm day is not nowhereland. The difference is the energy that's there.

You look for serendipity in nowhereland. It's one of the benefits of nowhereland. Lost serendipity can be found in nowhereland for those who have the skills and the courage to take a look. Nowhereland isn't for anybody, just like pioneering isn't for just anybody and settling isn't for everybody. It's not leaders and followers. It's just different skills.

The way the car is surging, it almost feels like it's starving for fuel or something is weird with the distributor — one of the two.

Since I started the trip, it's been sunny. All I do is squint. I can never find clip-on sunglasses that fit over my regular glasses. Well, last night I finally did at a truck stop. I'm so pleased. Today is a rainy, stormy day. I'll be damned. I'm going to wear my sunglasses anyway. So here I am in the rain and the only kid on the block wearing sunglasses. It just seems that sometimes there's no justice.

With all the newspaper clippings, "the renaissance man" has become a media superstar and a target. There's no representation of anything in this world that's honest. As soon as something is symbolized, as soon as something acquires a handle, a phrase, it no longer has anything to do with honesty. It only has to do with hype. There's nothing honest about just saying the same words over and over and over again.

These guys who go into nowhereland with their houses, it's like they don't want to take the risk associated with traveling in nowhereland, but they also are burdened by the liability of taking their houses and possessions into nowhereland. They might experience a real sense of loss if nowhere took their house from them. Travel with nothing at all in nowhereland or travel light and be willing to lose it.

74

I'd probably get better gas mileage if I took the parking brake off. Yes, you can go halfway across Nebraska with the parking brake on.

In Kearney, Nebraska, stopped at Boocaarts. Got so excited about how the thing was spelled that I drove into the parking lot over the curb in the sidewalk — to everybody's amazement. But the place can't be all that bad. They gave S&H Green Stamps.

Why is it that I'm feeling paranoid in this town — like it's me against them? I didn't mean to drive over their curb.

The town not only has cars driving on the streets, but also harvesters, tractors, and all sorts of ways of getting people around.

You should always travel in some way that it doesn't cost money to take your time.

There's all kinds of debris in the road. It takes some very skillful piloting to not run The Rattlesnake up on some of this shit.

Brave Rattlesnake. Not since Cousteau's Calypso has there been such a research vehicle to the pursuit of understanding.

The early Greeks thought up ways to think instead of looking in a particular way, saying in a particular way what they saw. That's why I like geology. It's exploration. You take a look and there it is or there it isn't. And then if you find something, you can just haul somebody else's ass out there to look at it too. Then you both can stand there with your hands in your pockets and say, "Yes, there it is. No doubt about it. That is there." As opposed to the experimentation and such that puts controls and one problem after another and observer impact on the experiment.

America has become about profiteering as opposed to pioneering.

People want ridiculous things at ridiculous prices as long as they're profiteering. They're living in a dream world of the profiteer and not in any sort of reality. Profiteers are slaves to the American dream. Mickey is profiteering for Disneyland.

There comes a time when you've got it together or you don't and you're faced with an opportunity to jump, the opportunity to go for it. Either you will or you won't. If the stakes are high enough, you'll go for it. You'll jump into the abyss.

Susan was deceitful with me every step of the way. I was an easy mark at that particular time. I'm of the notion that she never intended to follow through with any plans we made. She kept me hanging on. But no more. She wants two hundred and some dollars. She should be lucky I don't sue her and that poppy-headed boy-friend of hers for taking me to the cleaners. It doesn't matter the reason. It only matters the result.

As far as I'm concerned, she's just trying to keep me around as a consolation prize. If it doesn't work out with him, she's got a fallback position. I loved her. That's why it's especially painful to realize that she never loved me. She just used me — and is still trying to use me.

It became so blatantly apparent when you told me you were going to bring the frog and you couldn't even get your shit together to say goodbye, even over the tele-phone. You had your stuff out of storage, so goodbye, Michael. So piss off, Michael. I don't need you anymore.

There is no American reality except an outlaw reality. It's an outlaw reality because it doesn't contribute to the greater social good.

Just checked out the sculpture display at one of the Nebraska rest areas and it sure is a lot of money for a couple pieces of aluminum. Actually I liked the creaky windmill adjacent to the sculpture better.

"I am a DJ. I am what I play." — David Bowie.

Grappling with external forces is struggling with internal phantoms — internal demons that pop into a person's life. Demons hide behind the shield of virtue and right thinking and values. Devils wear white.

The big fear with myself, the one that was planted and reinforced by Joann is that there is no room in this world for people who are crazy. I'm not particularly crazy. I'm probably the sanest person I know, because I don't accept anything at face value. Yet there's a real loneliness and dread of loneliness of the alienation.

Be that as it may, we all travel alone anyway. I've tried it other ways and nothing worked. So what is left except to jump inside and take a journey?

In order to develop energy, you have to split apart electrons. Potential energy and the reuniting of the electrons, the flow of the electrons through the conduit is what does the work, that puts everything back into equilibrium. Kind of the same can be done by sitzing out away from yourself. You build up the same kind of energies. There has to be a point where it flows back together and you're reunited.

Only by looking at extremes can you figure out what's going on in the nonextreme. It could be just an extreme geology, but buried under a whole lot of alluvial fan.

The strongest structures are the ones that are bonded and interlocked and woven down to the molecular level. Everything is integrated. Not forged. Not manufactured. Not processed. But integrated from the ground up.

The Rattlesnake didn't like the intersection of 680 and 80 on the west side of Omaha. Didn't like it at all. Really put up a fuss. Whoa. I'm in the middle of tons of traffic.

Entering the world-famous tornado alley on a sultry afternoon with mucho cumulous clouds and hazy sunshine and humid weather. It's set up for a true disaster.

The road to Iowa is the gateway to agraria. This is different from the agrarian cultures in the West. First of all, there are no native agrarian cultures in the West, because there's no water out there, except what is transported. This is the birthplace of agraria.

Western agrarian cultures are driven not so much by the heritage of agraria, but rather by profiteering. Here we have a culture that goes back generation upon generation upon generation to the early 1800s at least. The natives here were agrarian.

The guy in the auto parts store wants to buy The Rattlesnake.

In some places, even when you see the horizon, it's a false horizon. You're looking at the tree line, not the true horizon.

The way to reach inside, to hunt for reality, is not by becoming reclusive. The pathway — the only way — to really dig down and do the charting is to reach out into the projection, into as many other projections as you can. And with that grand vocabulary of experiences and such, chart the map of your own reality.

Grandma Kleinschmidt pounded it into my father's head to make something out of himself. My dad bought it and made something out of himself, and he insisted on pounding it into my head. I wasn't aware at the time that my father and my mother had extensive conversations about how to deal with me, my father being just *so* disappointed that I would never settle down and do anything, whereas my mother kept saying, "Get off his back. He's going to do just fine." She was in my corner all the time.

It was that push to achieve that I just now … or maybe I haven't gotten rid of yet. I'm not enjoying as much as I could. The push to *make something out of* yourself. Like what? What's wrong with just *being* yourself?

When Grandpa Kleinschmidt retired, he did nothing but sit. They sold all the cows and Grandpa just sat. He sat and sat and sat. A month before the farm was to be sold and they were going to move into a little mobile home, on the way home from visiting us one day, he died. So he never had to move into a mobile home. The farm is a lot of space: 80 acres. A mobile home would put them together all the time. So he just died.

Survival of the fittest today may not be the case, because of radical changes in the environment. To base future expenditures on the future is stupid, because the future is not going to be the same as today. Things will change radically and without notice. I'm sure the dinosaur had a lot of plans.

A bunch of nuclear weapons go off and the nuclear winter is upon us and where's your career? Where are all your plans?

Good morning. Saturday the 16th.

Crows have been appearing to me during this entire trip. They appear at sunsets. And one just flew across the road in front of the car.

The objective is to feel the entire range of emotions. How much can I love somebody? How much can I hate somebody? How far can I push myself into chaos? How successful can I be by digging myself out?

People that run in the middle of the road are less alive. The fires don't burn quite as hot. But their meter is ticking.

Where's the life? Where's the fire? Where's that fire that consumes a person entirely, that envelops him in flames?

How much at the extremes of feeling, still keeping an even keel, do we experience? Extremes of emotions and it's like being in the big surf. The only way to survive is to kick back. Don't fight it. If you fight the emotions, you're going to die, boil up and crack. You gotta go with all that energy. If you hate somebody, you really gotta hate them. If you love somebody, you really gotta love them. If you hurt, you really gotta hurt. No holding back at all. You gotta go with the energy, just like in big surf.

Because we're on the road so much looking, it's to our advantage to learn how to have a good time on the road, as opposed to being so anxious to get somewhere.

Picture The Rattlesnake with a big parachute inflated in back of it and the driver is saying, "I can't understand why I'm getting lousy gas mileage."

I bought a cowboy hat — a disguise. When I walk into a bar, they won't know they are in the midst of a wooly-headed intellectual. Just a harmless, good ol' boy.

18th of June. Monday.

I'm in favor of preserving nature and the orderly flow and pace of change. But the flow changes nature, so pace is what we have to get in tune with, whether it is orderly or not.

The only thing you can hide from is yourself. I don't have any desire to go backward, so I keep a line of sight forward. What I want is the broadest line of sight and to develop peripheral vision so if I can see something that's interesting, I can stop and look at it. Some people don't look out at all. But they're still moving, and they're not paying any attention to the obstacles they might run into.

What an intense weekend. Started with arriving in Madison and the note on the door that Kate and Tom were not going to be around. Then going to the 602, wrote a letter to Julie and drank beer. Then to Tammy's house and sitting and talking with Kate, listening to her talk about Miami, her life, the whole works. And Tammy showing up. First called Dick and let him know I was coming. Then I called Amy and Rich to find out what their plans were. Dinner at six. Then called Dick back and made plans for 8 o'clock on Sunday. Sat, drank beer until a quarter to 3. Went over to listen to Kate talk. Tammy showed up and we sat around and talked some more. Then after taking showers and stuff, we had gin and tonics and went over to Rich and Amy's and then went to the Indian restaurant and then back to Rich and Amy's house and drank a bottle of whiskey. Then we went out. Kate drove. We went to the 602. Walked up and down State Street and then went to Tammy's house. Next morning, Kate and I went to the lab. Met Brian. I went for a walk while she cleaned out her office. After that, we went out and had coffee. Took a picture of her and went back to Tammy's house. She packed. Brian came over, picked up Kate and took her to the airport. Then Tammy and I talked until the sun went down. She went to the store, and I went to sleep.

I went out to visit Ryan and Marsha and then Angie and then went back to Tammy's. This morning, Tammy went to work and I laid around the house until I got together with Amy. Went out to lunch. Said goodbye to Amy, then went over to Babcock Hall. Got ice cream. Went to the lab. Talked with Tammy. Went to coffee with Rich. Took a picture of him. Said goodbye. Went with Tammy to the union. We talked for a couple hours. Said good-bye, got in car, left town. Here I am.

Magic is generated at the source, not in the projection.

In the group of humans that sat down and invented fire, there was one genius. It comes down to one person sitting down — one very flexible person without bounds, without preconceptions — to figure out how something works. Everybody else can copycat if they please, unless they can come up with something better.

The biologist argues that humans took off when they began to communicate and the anthropologist argues that human evolution went into high gear when they began shaping tools.

Toni says, "I wish you hadn't told me that about your-self." Question to her is, "Did you want me to keep it a secret? Did you want me to feed an illusion or present facts?"

If an individual goes to the place that's the subject of the investigation, lives there, keeps their own accounts and their own points of view and does a firsthand account of what's there objectively, there's much less energy involved and they have complete control of how the account is filed. If more individuals would do that, then the messages would be far more powerful than having a group of individuals on a Sunday afternoon getting out and chanting and waving their flags in the hope that their message will be carried — and be carried accurately — to people making decisions.

There are many problems with being inflexible and hanging onto certain ideals as being *the* way — the *right* way.

I'm not an expert on either point of view. However, I do know what I see. And I can interpret what I see and what I experience in the field.

Going to school, I'll just pick up what I can on the run. Because to put anything on hold is contrary to my meter running, which makes me very uneasy. It's like getting ready to do something, rather than just doing it with all its ragged edges. The only person that's going to be taking the risks is me. And the only person that benefits is me. And I have to keep referring to my track record of accomplishments.

Mine is not the way of the warrior. It's the way of the tourist, the way of the mapmaker.

0610 hrs 21 June. Summer solstice.

On my way to Colorado.

The hardest thing about traveling is leaving.

The goal is to not be astounded or appalled at anything, but to celebrate everything.

I dream of an illusive reality that's not attainable in a dream, yet the dream is the benchmark. The dream is the pathway.

I don't believe in magic, because that's an internal thing generated out of reality. But I do believe in miracles.

Crossing the time zone from east to west and driving during the summer solstice, I'm going to see more sunshine than most people can in one day.

Can you jump a timing chain and compensate for it with your distributor? Interesting question.

Flash flood warnings up around Sioux City. That's why I didn't take the northern route.

The technology that allows the bourgeoisie to have time to worry about social issues is the technology that is killing them. Using up energy. If everybody had to farm their own stuff and not shop in a grocery store, the social concerns would be secondary to environmental concerns. It's especially true in the industrial north, where urban survival of winters is absolutely dependent on transportation of food and fuel.

Things haven't always been the way they are, and this won't last. That's guaranteed.

Social consciousness is a product of communication, which is a product of technology. You don't grow paper; you grow trees. Think of all the processes that go into just communicating in print.

There's a hazard with semis passing. I'll be tooling along at 50 miles per hour and a semi will come past and pull right in front of me and all of the sudden I'm sucked in behind him and The Rattlesnake just starts going crazy because I'm not bucking the wind anymore. I can't even back out without The Rattlesnake going crazy.

It looks really dark up north. This may have been a very smart idea ducking south of Des Moines. That remains to be seen; we're not through it yet. I'll be happy when Omaha is in my rearview mirror.

The weather looks really gnarly to the east and to the north. I just might have missed it.

Sixty miles north of Des Moines.

Science runs on assumptions. Assuming that a reputable person does reputable work and basing conclusions in your work on their paper and assuming that their work was OK and assuming that other people's work was OK and basing your reputation and conclusions on their work plus yours, which your work might be OK, but theirs? You're assuming they did a good job.

Leaving people is something you never get used to.

Before 5 o'clock. I've gotten through Des Moines, heading for Council Bluffs and one or two clouds in the sky. Clear sailing. So far, so good.

Think small, but think a lot.

Western Iowa is much like western Wisconsin.

About 80 miles east of Omaha, all of the sudden, the sky just turned black to the north of me. Talk about a line of storms. I hope it isn't moving south.

Well, looks like I'm driving through a bunch of tornadoes. Not quite made it to Omaha. This whole big line of shit just came screaming down from the north. The radio says there are funnel clouds all over the place. Lucky me.

The Rattlesnake is starting to overheat again. Oh boy.

I hate Iowa.

Suddenly the air temperature dropped 10 degrees. The snake stopped overheating and I'm still in the middle of these things. 6:30. At least it will be cooler once this thing moves through.

It's windier than hell out there. On the radio, they just said there are tornadoes all over the place. It's a quarter till. I'm driving under a funnel cloud. Tremendous rain, tremendous wind.

Ten minutes to 7. Shelby is ahead. I'm 35 miles from Council Bluffs.

It's raining like a sonofabitch. It's six minutes to 7.

South of Audubon County and northern Cass County is where they're spotting the funnel clouds in western Iowa.

From the time it was sunny outside and I saw the clouds coming until now was an hour.

Poor Rattlesnake just isn't running well. Another storm ahead loaded with lightning.

With this load, the snake rides like a truck.

Back on the road at 8:30. There's always that possibility we might have the problem licked with the snake. Not the rattle. The rattle will be there forever. But it seems the inside of the distributor cap was a problem. The contacts had a layer of plastic on them, apparently causing the thing to be way out of time. Of course, if it's out of time, it runs hot. I corrected a little bit by changing the timing on it, but then apparently the whole thing got coated with plastic right in the middle of the tornado storm, just when I needed the car. Now it seems to be running pretty good. It hasn't gotten warm yet at all. We'll see.

Driving into a sunset. I'm so cool, I have to wear my sunglasses.

During the entire storm, the CB didn't work.

Traveling alone is a real bitch, because you haven't got any co-pilot to help you out with coffee and putting tapes in the recorder and picking out the tapes and figuring out where the radio is. It's difficult trying to do that and drive at the same time.

How come the girl in the Happy Chef restaurant insists on pushing the stainless steel cup onto the top of the Thermos, rather than twisting it on the way it was designed?

Computers can only think without compassion. Animals are completely compassionate without being able to "think." It's the human that has both pathways.

Social arguments and conceptual arguments, politically correct arguments are polarized. Polarities are resolved through conflict, as opposed to the ordered ebb and flow that is found in nature or that *is* nature.

22 June, past 4 a.m.

The girl, when she did my coffee last night, did every-thing so perfect. She preseasoned the pot — the whole works — and then jammed the lid on.

At 0430 hours, it's foggy here in central Nebraska.

It's 0530. It's daybreak, muggy and warm. I'm running headlong into an electrical storm about 25 to 30 miles down the road. I wish the CB worked.

0630. Just a couple miles east of North Platte.

7 in the morning. The sun it out. Clear skies. The snake is running good. It likes clear skies and sunshine as we blast into western Nebraska, heading for Colorado.

The Rattlesnake sure does draw a crowd at rest stops, especially from old people. They really like to look at it. You'd think these people never saw a snake before. What's embarrassing isn't that it is unusual. What's embarrassing is the attention other people pay to it, as if it's the only rattlesnake they've ever seen in their lives.

I must be hallucinating from lack of sleep, because different components on the dashboard seem to be fluid and bouncing independent from what the rest of the car is doing. This thing really rides like a truck. I guess the gauges, instead of being mounted with screws, were mounted on springs. Wow.

It's 9:30 Mountain Time and I'm just about at Sterling, Colorado, about 20 miles out of Denver. The air is warm. Skies are clear. The snake is running good.

Got a new antenna, but the CB still doesn't work; so I'm going to try a new power supply.

In Sterling, I was looked at real suspiciously by a cop. This is the sort of rig that law enforcement officers don't like to see come off the freeway into their cute little towns, molesting their women and consuming their goods.

Couple of batteries and short-circuited the whole car electrical system. Bypassed the car electrical system so I could use the CB.

Now that I got the CB fixed, I know where all the police are.

The snake has a new trick: right after fueling pulling out on the freeway and dying once, dying twice. Like somebody just pulls the plug. Then it runs until the next time I get gas. But that's the way snakes are.

With these polarized sunglasses, if I tip my head to the side, the sky lightens up. If I tip my head back, the sky gets dark. It's real psychedelic. Makes the clouds stand out. Makes the Rocky Mountains stand out too.

With these glasses, I'm looking at the world through polarized eyes. It's a polarized dream. One way it's light. They next way it's dark. Horizon is light. Horizon is dark. Mountains are light. Mountains are dark.

A lot of horizon out here. A lot of nothing out here. About 40 miles east of Denver.

There's a Stuckey's.

The sky turns light and dark as I turn my head. It appears the ground does just the opposite. But I betcha it's an optical illusion caused by association. I have to watch out for these horizons. It's really difficult. You know where the line is, but what's happening on top and on bottom is anybody's guess. It's all special effects. It's all a dream. The line is the only thing that's real.

What is above and below the horizon line is all a dream. And polarized, depending on what lenses you are wearing, much like social and political polarization and energy — whatever is polarized by whatever ideals a person chooses to look through. The effect of the observer on the observed. Except the horizon line. It's the only thing that doesn't change. The only "change" the horizon line undergoes is because of changes in point of view. You change the point of view and the horizon line *apparently* changes. That's why the map is so important: so that you establish a point of view and come back to it, look at it, and chart the pathway to reality — a reality that you keep pushing away. But by pushing it away and expanding the horizon line, making the horizon line bigger and fuller, you come to grips with it. You understand it.

People on the road here don't even notice there is a horizon line. When a person is seasick, what do they have to focus on? The horizon. When a dream is so bizarre that even your body gets screwed up, the only place to focus is on the horizon line — on that reality. The map is so important to understanding the horizon line.

A lot of times, objects that obscure the horizon appear to be something they're not, like that car that pulled up in back of me that looked like it had two bubble-gum machines on top of it and me and The Rattlesnake had to behave ourselves and it turned out to be to be a full-size sedan pulling a trailer with two posts sticking up out of the trailer. From the silhouette, you would have sworn it was the highway patrol.

The truck driver on the CB calls something a space station. It must be a motor home. Talking about going in to eat. Driving his truck and he got bored. Went in to eat. Came out and jabbered on the radio and talked to the space station.

Some maneuvers on the road could be recommended. Some aren't. One that isn't is changing film in the camera while passing another car. There's just a whole lot of attention that needs to be paid to all kinds of things.

Theory on why the car heated up all of the sudden yesterday is that it lost the diaphragm to the advance mechanism. When I pushed the distributor forward or advanced the spark about 6 degrees, things fell in line. Now it's running OK, but it doesn't idle worth a shit.

90

By turning my head with the music, I can make the clouds dance and make the horizon line change its character, however not its position, its color.

Are humans the only source who can make structures at their will? Animals burrow hills, but they don't make structures. What they do is evacuate material. They create structures in essence by removing materials. We made structures by manipulating materials and changing them from one thing to another.

Plans are just talk, no matter how serious or well founded they are. They have nothing to do with what's happening right now.

In Denver. 1 p.m.

There's only one way to enter metropolis: Crank up the CB, crank up the radio, crank up the snake. Just jam through. Run a lap with the tape recorder in hand. Oldies on the radio. Get all those things going for you and just live your way through it.

Losing power in the middle of downtown Denver. Car didn't stop completely. It is too weird. It seems to be starving for fuel.

Three lights down to Federal. Turn left. Five blocks on the left-hand side. Auto parts store.

It's five minutes to 3 and we're rolling. The Rattlesnake seems to be running OK and did the shift without losing its distinctive rattle. Everybody in traffic is trying to get me. I'm not nervous.

On the freeway. Running OK. Bumper to bumper traffic in the other lane. The CB is running. Everything is running.

I'm not an optimist; I'm just skillful. I'm even starting to like the rattle.

Think I'll drink beer tonight.

Pulling into Denver, taking pictures of downtown, listening to tunes when all of the sudden the car starts bucking and starving for fuel. That's all right. I can handle that. It did it a little bit before. Ended up pulling off right by Mile High Stadium. Ran OK in the streets. Back on the freeway. Starve, starve. People beeping their horns at me. I'm doing 25; they're doing 100. Grab the next exit. There's a Standard station and a park. Pulled into the park. Walked to the Standard station. Asked where there's an auto parts store. Got in the car and headed for the auto parts store. Didn't make it. Car died. Walked five blocks to the auto parts store. Got the part, brought it back, put it in. Blew out the fuel line just in case. Never can tell. This living stuff — once you get it down, it's all right.

That's not true.

Completely fogbound, snowblind, or with your eyes closed and blindfolded, you can identify the horizon line. In order to figure out how to get there, you don't Zen out. You don't sitz out. You drop in. You embrace the dream with everything you've got.

Clouds to the west. More storms coming in.

It's suspicious how, after fueling and sitting in a rest area, the car would choke a little bit and then run OK. I think the fuel pump was all right. I think I just had a piece of crud floating around in the gas tank. It's just a matter of paying attention to what's happening in the dream. You never know when you're going to use those little bits and pieces of information you collect.

Leaving Denver on city streets, The Rattlesnake was really feeling his oats.

Where am I? I'm out of town, that's all I know. I hope I'm on the right road.

Car on the side of the road with a woman walking away. Some people aren't as fortunate in their breakdowns. A polite car will always break down near an auto parts store.

Colorado Springs, socked into some hotrod traffic here. Good thing I'm bailing off this interstate.

The snake is running like shit. Can't go up the hill that way, so cleaned the distributor cap and sparkplugs. They were all beginning to be foul. Found one that was completed fouled. Rejetted the carburetor for this altitude. I'm going to fill up with gasoline and should be able to make the run for home.

I need to find a gas station. Rattles. Very tired, by the way.

Five o'clock and I got about 50 miles of mountain roads ahead of me.

I love being in the mountains. This is just gorgeous.

Signs say in case of flash flood climb to safety. The traffic here is doing 25. It's a real climb.

Now everybody's down to 15, and I don't mind at all.

I think all these people lined up on the road are waiting for the Olympic torch. This is too much.

Going up this hill and I see all these people looking toward the west and I put two and two together that the Olympic torch is coming through here. Now all of the sudden the CB lights up: Olympic torch this, Olympic torch that. Of course, I've got exposed film in the camera, so now I have to change the film while driving up this mountain road.

Just when the two roads come together and I'm right next to the other lane, the runner comes trotting by and the sun comes out. So I'm able to increase my depth of field so I can take pictures. It's nice of them to arrange this for me.

Getting up where it's hard to breathe.

5:20 is when the runner came scootin' by and now its 5:26.

It's hard to believe we did it. What a run, huh?

Down to the last leg of the road to reality. I'll tidy up my act in terms of packing the snake and the last leg will be done in real style.

Ain't gonna like going down this hill. It's big. It's long. It's about 4,000 feet of elevation over about 30 miles.

Man, I'm glad I bought new tires.

The view of Cripple Creek from the road overlooking it is just spectacular. Gold mines here.

It's Sunday evening, 10 after 10 p.m. I'm heading up the hill out of Cripple Creek. The sky is clear. The stars are big. The air is clean. I feel good. The car feels good. This is the last leg.

I've learned how to work in Los Angeles. Now I have to learn how to make Los Angeles work for me.

After crashing in a rest area about an hour, 5:30 to 6:30, pulled out of the rest area and the car immediately overheated. No water in the radiator, a big crack in the top tank. Took all the water I had with me. Got it cooled down and back on the road with a little water in the radiator. OK so far. Not running any harder than 45 miles per hour.

A lot of people assume that reality is the same for each person. Reality is absolutely unique to every individual.

I sure do love Volkswagens; they don't have radiators.

Getting to Arcosanti causes overheating. Such is the way of the chase for living and horizons. I think I'll spend the night in Flagstaff in a motel where I can work on my notes, be quiet, take a shower. Or I'll just go shopping in Flagstaff and pick out a cozy rest area and have something to eat, maybe work with my notes a little bit and go to sleep when it gets dark.

I'll have breakfast tomorrow in Arcosanti.

I'm taking it easy with the car, hanging right in there about 50. Easier on the car; easier on me.

The lonely cowboy talking to his comrades on the CB.

Towns in Arizona are really out in the middle of nowhere.

Thanks to truckers, I avoided a big accident.

A girl on a bicycle with leotards and tights coming back from her exercise class. The school in Flagstaff is Northern Arizona University.

Bought some Bar's Leaks, none of that fancy crap they tried to sell me. Pinched over the seams on the radiator.

As soon as I get to a rest area, I'll put in the Bar's Leaks and should be in good shape for the rest of the run.

Out of Flagstaff. It's all downhill the rest of the way.

Beautiful sunset heading out of Flagstaff. Been on the road maybe, oh, 20 miles. Car's running great. Got it to stop leaking. Fueled up. Got myself a pint of strawberry ice cream. Listening to classical music. Doesn't come any better than this. Going through the pines. About 6,000 feet, heading for Arcosanti.

It's an *Arizona Magazine* sunset.

Radiator blew out, but it's apparently under control now.

I've got about 320 miles to Los Angeles.

Radiator just blew out again. 22 miles from Chorus Junction. As many times as I've blown out this radiator, I'm surprised I haven't blown a head gasket.

Ringer they threw in. This hill is steeper than the one outside Salt Lake City. I doubt whether it's as long, but it sure is as steep. Definitely a reason why I like Volkswagens and stick shifts.

Good morning. It's Tuesday morning about 3 a.m. There's a big rest area about eight miles south of Chorus Junction. I don't even want to get into a discussion of brakes on this thing.

Going down this hill, I've got one foot on the gas slightly to keep the rattle from going crazy and one foot on the brake.

I just kicked it into neutral and when I start to apply the brake, the thing pulls wildly to the right. When I compensate, when I let go of the brake, the thing careens to the left.

Linkage on the transmission is such that trying to put it back into drive sometimes I miss and stick it in first.

Coming down into the desert, the air that was so nice and cool and kept the snake running cool is getting warm. It's 3 o'clock in the morning, and it's about 85 degrees out.

It's the end of the last leg. Talk about taking it easy. Going up hills, going 25 to 30 mph, not putting any strain on the engine. Trying to keep the radiator intact. Going down hills 45ish. Now we got another big hill. Got to back way off. It's just going to take a while.

My timing for running through Phoenix will be good, about 4:30 in the morning. Looking down in the valley, the line of lights on the horizon is Phoenix.

Haven't begun to talk about the headlights that flick on and off with the voltage regulator.

I can smell all the crud burning off my engine, all the radiator crud.

Chorus Junction was a real madhouse last night about 10 or 11 o'clock — a combination of truck drivers and architecture students, mostly female.

Had a beer, my eyeballs frazzled from driving, trying to keep my car together.

Two hills, two mounds of dirt that rise out of the horizon. Each has a red light flashing on top.

Will see if I can just roll through town and pick up fuel on the other side.

Trucks with hay bales just came zipping past me.

Just drove past a sign that says it's 4:16 a.m., 86 degrees.

Pickup trucks going by with dogs in the back barking at everything, including the snake.

Local traffic section in Phoenix. Ready to stop for gas and hook up with the freeway. It's daybreak.

I didn't blow out the radiator. I just boiled out the radiator. There was no water left in it at all. A credit to the snake. She can run on just nothing. As long as there's any water circulating at all, the thing will run.

If memory serves me, there are no gas stations on the west side of Phoenix, no matter how badly you want one.

Boy, situation after situation. Now I'm out here expecting full well to at least come across a gas station and there isn't one. Pushing it up the hill and all the sudden blowing it up. Everything would be OK if it wasn't for situations.

It's hard to tell if the smells are the snake boiling over or all the crops in the area, because it all smells the same.

There are no more hills, no more mountains, until I get to Los Angeles.

About five miles looking for a gas station and with only a gallon of water in there, the cooling system is hanging together so far.

I'm in the desert, so I can tell I'm getting close to being home. Looks like Coachella. It isn't Coachella, but it looks like Coachella.

Remind myself never to have these kind of tangled wires again. Everything is tangled up.

Make sure the model works, because the energy goes from useful to useless. It does not ever disappear. I'm saying that energy can be created and destroyed by ego.

Just lost another hour trying to get this car heat under control. 6 o'clock and I'm still just outside Phoenix. Radiator blew up. Blew everything all over the engine again. The engine came completely unglued. I'm going to have to keep the cap off, stop every 30 miles, whenever, put water in it, take it easy the last 200 miles. I'll be damned if I'm going to continue my career as a mechanic. I'll just be damned.

When I think about getting around and what it takes to get somewhere and just the energy it takes to maintain getting around, getting other people's asses around, no way.

Running rough again. Temperature is starting to come up. I only went one mile.

Another thing The Rattlesnake likes to do is jump into gear and run me over. The way it stands, it still leaks. Soldered it, still leaks, and I'm going 45 miles per hour. I'll see if I can just get through and keep checking the water every opportunity and see if I can nurse it to Thermal. Keeping my fingers crossed.

Radiator blew up again.

Down to a couple of pinholes. I tried to seal just squeezing it shut with a screwdriver. May have worked. Now I need to get to water, I hope for the last time.

All I've got to do is just keep the radiator together and everything is ducky.

Now I filled it up with coolant so it won't boil over. I did a road repair, soldering a big crack in the radiator. I'm on the road, about 100 miles to Blythe.

I think I put so much sealer in this engine that every time it blew out, the residue cooked onto the engine and now it's not thermal conducting like it ought to.

What's important: parachute packs, cars, tools, notes.

The way it stands, 50 miles east of Blythe, run about 10 miles, pour a little water over the radiator and I can run another 10 miles. I'm able to run at about 55.

It's 9:30 a.m.

The business I want to be in is running a truck stop.

It doesn't matter how well the machine works. It just matters that you keep popping off miles, one mile at a time.

Persistence is the key that unlocks doors, not any kind of packaging or experience, skills, or any of that kind of stuff. Just persistence. It's frustrating sometimes, but you never give up.

I know I'm close to home when I see bumper stickers advertising Hussong's.

Overheating. It's 11 o'clock. All I've got to do is get 15 more miles, and I may not make it.

The radiator is hanging together. Stuff isn't boiling over too bad. It's running hot. It's running, but it just isn't getting cool. I mean, it's not that hot outside. It just refuses to get cool.

Have to cool it off now. I can't get it to even come down below the hot line. Used to be I could get it at least down a little ways. Six miles to the rest area.

There's so much pressure in the radiator that I blew up another seam. Fortunately, this is all downhill.

Going downhill and it's heating up.

Dumping water over the heads, over the radiator, over everything. The needle won't even come off of hot at all.

Turned the engine off and I'm coasting down the hill. I don't know how smart that is.

As I was pumping gas after this whole ordeal with the radiator, checking out thermostats, all that kind of stuff, with a whole carful of tools, a Mexican guy at a gas station didn't have enough money to pay for his gas and wanted to sell me a box of tools.

I'm driving into Blythe at 12:30 p.m. The temperature is about 110 to 115, with a car that's overheating.

You never realize how important water is — not only to the car, to me, to everything, because the entire value of the cargo is dependent on securing a couple of canteens and a cooler full of water to make this trip across the desert. Still have 100 miles to go.

At that stop, I checked the thermostat. Then I flushed the radiator, the cooling system, and got all the crud out of it. Filled up with fuel, got some Cokes.

Now if the car overheats, I have a fighting chance to cool it down again.

Five miles outside of Blythe. As I drop down into Blythe, I feel the temperature pick up another five degrees. It is hot out there.

Got some coolant pulling out of Blythe. Five minutes to 1 o'clock. I'm sure it's 118 out here.

Why go across the desert now? Because I really want to see Cindy tonight.

Gas station at the top of the hill outside of Blythe. Came in and the water was disconnected for about a half-hour. Opened up the hood. Took 20 minutes for it to cool down. Checked how much water I lost. Most of that I lost in boiling after I shut the motor off. Just about a little bit of the tank, maybe a pint. It was running pretty hot, but seemed to be running and keeping the water in there. So what I'm going to do is drive in 20-mile stints. I've got about 80 miles to go, so that would be four stops. I can deal with that. I hope there are no hills.

I've encountered a bit of a headwind. The wind blowing on my arm burns it. How can I expect it to cool my poor, precious snake's motor?

Talk about shimmering desert horizons. It's hot.

When I back off the gas and the snake rattles, the temperature also drops a little bit. Let it rattle.

The rattle was annoying in the beginning, but now I love that rattle.

What value is placed on which dreams? How do we make decisions?

Pathways to reality are through an individual's mind and body together, not to take the jump into reality but take the jump inside by using the dreams to find reality on the pathways.

There are many roads to reality and many maps. It gets down to a matter of value and choice. How do you want to go about it, if at all?

I set up this run across the desert as being through the furnace and through hell and demons and things. The road to reality is occupied not only by people who encourage, but also sorts that discourage at every opportunity.

Demons come in the forms of other people. They come in the forms of experiences.

I have to get a newspaper for how hot it was today. I don't have to worry about coffee getting cold. The demons don't realize that.

At Desert Center, I'll let it cool down and see how much water I've used.

The most nothing is in California. Less than 200 miles from the most something, which is Los Angeles. Everything else in the country is kind of spread out evenly.

A dust devil just came swirling by.

Value is the application of reality and dreams: mind, body, and heart.

Took a half-hour nap at the cooling-off place.

Motor home that cuts you off, barely sneaks by and then slows down. You just watch the old needle go right to hot. That was on a pull for Chiraco Summit. Chiraco Summit is downhill all the way.

Over the summit, even the snake cooled down a little bit. It's the first time it's ever gone backwards this whole run across the desert.

Box Canyon Road overpass on I-10.

The road to reality has two lanes: one going and one coming.

Because we can see the road from a distance doesn't mean we can travel on it. We just may not have the equipment to do it. However, some of us need more sophisticated equipment than others because we don't have the skills to take less sophisticated equipment on the road.

The energy goes into getting the equipment for the road rather than keeping the equipment on the road.

To show how defiant I am to the demons, I should make a run right through the heart of hell: Box Canyon Road.

The snake gave out his rattle in defiance, saying, "Yeah, we can't be had."

Even a wild piece of American geology isn't too much for the Snake and Four Eyes.

Coming up the canyon, giant blast furnace.

Only 10 miles to go and another leg completed. This is to be savored.

Hot rubber on the tires, the swaying front end, and there before us was the Salton Sea, 234 feet below sea level. We had conquered them all. We had flown to the sky and we'd gone through the heart of hell into the bowels of the Earth.

Less than five miles. The snake is rattling like crazy. It is so steep and so downhill. The air is 118 degrees, 40 miles per hour. The radiator wouldn't dare overheat now. I've got so much water packed in this thing, it doesn't stand a chance. Demons away.

It is our job to seek harmony, to get rid of the good, get rid of the bad, get rid of energy, get rid of structure, get rid of everything and be at peace, finally, for one and for all, until some little bit of ego comes along and the whole thing starts all over again. An entirely different place within an entirely different time. All the rules start from scratch. The gift of harmony is the option to be a universe unto yourself and to remain at peace.

It's a choice we have to wait for. It's a choice that every individual has today, every moment, with every breath they take.

Every spirit is a universe unto itself, but with one extra special feature — that is we can dream.

We carry the reality with us, but we are able to dream. We are able to project. We are able to experiment, to learn, to build. We can only do that as human beings. We can never ever do this again once we're dead.

Every minute, every moment, the meter is ticking. We are on the clock. Every breath. There is only today, the road to reality. Every individual heart is on that road every day. Unfortunately, they don't know it.

Arriving in Mecca at Chuck and Pam's, five minutes before 4 in the afternoon, 26 June, 1984. A couple of days of R&R.

I hope I took the right turn.

This is not right. I missed. In the vineyards, I took the wrong turn. I've only been here a thousand other times.

Wednesday the 27th. Traveling the pathways of a dream in search of reality.

Good morning, 29th of June.

Friday 6 a.m., temperature about 80 degrees. Just left Charlie's; on my way to Los Angeles.

After 20 minutes, by the time I got to Indio, the temperature was over half and on its way to boiling over.

Got gas in Palm Desert. It only lost just a little bit of water.

As The Rattlesnake and I climb up to Banning Pass, my thoughts are on the abyss ahead. The journey is nearly finished, and now comes the scary part. Take what I learned, jump into the abyss and find new landmarks. Go exploring uncharted turf. Sneak into the water slowly, get a feel for the territory. Once it's familiar, I can easily get back to the same places and chart it.

But the jump isn't out toward the horizon. In order to reach the horizon, you have to jump inside, because the pathways are the mind and body.

How well can we deal with what we've projected and what other people have projected? How flexible can we remain searching for new landmarks, and how skillful can we become and how articulately can we plant our benchmarks?

If we search outside of ourselves, we'll never find the answers. The only place we can look for the answers is inside, because that's where reality lies. That's where the harmony lies. That's where the real horizons are.

Pushing back horizons is merely pushing back our own limitations. To confront the fears, the monsters, the demons that dwell within us.

You never conquer the ocean, because the ocean is unconquerable. In mountain climbing, you can never conquer the mountain, because the mountain is unconquerable. The only thing you can conquer is yourself, your own fears, your own misgivings, your own rigid attitudes.

The jump isn't into tangles of freeways, buildings of steel and glass, and people whose projections can only be best described as dangling on the end of a yo-yo.

As I approach the Banning summit, the air is turning orange and I can smell smog from the city just on the other side.

A couple of times, the car conked out short of Banning Pass. But everything is under control. It didn't boil over seriously.

The other side of the pass, The Rattlesnake signaled its disapproval at this whole idea by running warm and rattling its engine. The snake doesn't want to be here. The snake knows what's ahead isn't easy for it either.

Rest area. The air is cool. The temperature of the car is settling down.

I've clipped the extra set of keys on my key ring: my storage locker, to Lola's house, to my mailboxes, all that stuff. Gave the snake a last drink of water before heading down the hill and turning on the tape. "Hotel California."

Traffic begins to pick up. It's 20 minutes after 8 o'clock.

It makes me very sad that this trip is over. It was a good one.

Coming down the hill, I'm just savoring the images. Beautiful things and people I met and saw.

Rialto is the last rest area on I-10 before you get into Los Angeles.

West Covina dead ahead down into the smog, ducking debris on the freeway.

The trip is over. 10:25 a.m. 29 June, 1984, intersection of Santa Monica and the San Diego freeways.

This town sucks.

The snake had so many holes in the radiator after I fixed it that it steam-cleaned the crud off the motor.

Rent-a-Car was unloading four car carriers into an empty lot. It looks like they're stocking up for the Olympics. All the same cars.

www.ingramcontent.com/pod-product-compliance
Lightning Source LLC
Chambersburg PA
CBHW071212220526
45468CB00002B/576